Using EQUITY AUDITS in the CLASSROOM to Reach and Teach All Students

Using EQUITY AUDITS in the CLASSROOM

to Reach and Teach All Students

KATHRYN BELL McKENZIE • LINDA SKRLA

Foreword by Christine Sleeter

CORWIN
A SAGE Company

A SAGE Company

FOR INFORMATION:

SAGE Publications, Inc.
2455 Teller Road
Thousand Oaks, California 91320
E-mail: order@sagepub.com

SAGE Publications Ltd.
1 Oliver's Yard
55 City Road
London, EC1Y 1SP
United Kingdom

SAGE Publications India Pvt. Ltd.
B 1/I 1 Mohan Cooperative Industrial Area
Mathura Road, New Delhi 110 044
India

SAGE Publications Asia-Pacific Pte. Ltd.
33 Pekin Street #02-01
Far East Square
Singapore 048763

Acquisitions Editor: Arnis Burvikovs
Associate Editor: Desirée A. Bartlett
Editorial Assistant: Kimberly Greenberg
Production Editors: Cassandra Margaret Seibel and Veronica Stapleton
Copy Editor: Cate Huisman
Typesetter: Hurix Systems
Proofreader: Susan Schon
Indexer: Gloria Tierney
Cover Designer: Anthony Paular
Permissions Editor: Karen Ehrmann

Copyright © 2011 by Corwin

Printed in the United States of America.

Library of Congress Cataloging-in-Publication Data

McKenzie, Kathryn Bell.

Using equity audits in the classroom to reach and teach all students/Kathryn Bell McKenzie, Linda Skrla; foreword by Christine Sleeter.

p. cm

Includes bibliographical references and index.

ISBN 978-1-4129-8677-9 (pbk.)

1. School improvement programs—United States. 2. Educational equalization—United States—Evaluation. 3. Effective teaching—United States. 4. Classroom environment—United States. I. Skrla, Linda, 1957– II. Title.

LB2822.82.M39 2011

379.2'60973—dc22

2010054608

This book is printed on acid-free paper.

11 12 13 14 15 10 9 8 7 6 5 4 3 2 1

Contents

Foreword

Christine Sleeter

I wish I had this book 20 years ago! At that time, after having learned to identify institutionalized patterns of discrimination in schools that can be changed, two colleagues and I tried to help teachers in four schools analyze their own schools and classrooms. We developed a package of data collection tools designed to guide their investigation into patterns such as race and class backgrounds of students in academic tracks or ability groups, race and gender representation in the curriculum, race/gender patterns of interaction in classrooms, and gaps between teaching styles teachers used and those students preferred (Sleeter, 1992). For a year, teachers in the four schools gathered mountains of data.

Gradually, however, two problems became apparent. First, the amount of data that had been gathered far exceeded the time teachers had to analyze it. My sense about what data were relevant had been guided by my experience conducting ethnographic studies in schools, and as a result, we far overshot what was manageable. Rather than helping teachers focus attention on a few key factors they could address, we overwhelmed them. Second, we realized that we lacked a process to help the teachers "make the familiar seem strange" so that they could think differently about problems they took for granted and ineffective "solutions" they were used to. As data they managed to analyze suggested patterns that we believed should be confronted, such as disproportionate disciplinary referrals of African American students, we realized that the teachers did not necessarily see themselves as able to address or responsible for addressing those patterns.

In *Using Equity Audits in the Classroom to Reach and Teach All Students*, McKenzie and Skrla offer a clearly focused, highly usable set of tools that enable teachers to pinpoint and begin to address central equity problems in classrooms. McKenzie and Skrla are very well versed on the range of persistent inequities based on race, gender, language, and disability that are deeply embedded in the structures and practices of schooling. But they are also pragmatic change agents. The brilliance of this book is that, by beginning with the question of who is actively engaged in your classroom and who is not, and by identifying the evidence you are using to assess students' engagement, the authors make use of your professional knowledge and honor your ability to think through problems when guided in asking and reflecting on the right questions. In a sense, this book offers a tool for teachers that models forms of teaching that most contribute to student learning.

Hattie's (2009) comprehensive meta-analysis of research evidence highlights the predominant influence of the teacher on student achievement. Specifically, teachers whose students achieve academically seek feedback from their students regarding what the students know and understand, and where they are confused and are making errors. Such teachers have a clear understanding of what they want students to learn and what learning looks like, and they can guide the students interactively, providing regular feedback. *Using Equity Audits in the Classroom to Reach and Teach All Students* zeroes in on a problem teachers care about— students they are not reaching. Although McKenzie and Skrla are not working personally with you, through this book they engage you in active investigation into your own practice, interacting with you along the way.

To be sure, this book does not take on the wide range of inequities in schools and the wider society. School curricula, for example, are generally based on the worldview of members of the dominant society. Many students in urban classrooms come to school from communities that are systematically oppressed through racist housing patterns, an absence of good jobs, routine racial profiling, and ongoing violence (McCarthy, Crichlow, Dimitriadis, & Dolby, 2005). Despite these huge and persistent problems, however, McKenzie and Skrla challenge us to break the link between academic achievement and students' racial, gender, language, disability, and social class backgrounds. Breaking that link, in itself, matters greatly to students, and it is doable. I recall watching the same groups of students in a diverse, urban secondary school move from one classroom to the next, encountering markedly different experiences from one teacher to the next. While one teacher found most of the students unteachable and poorly behaved, the next teacher engaged the very same students in worthwhile academic learning. Teachers have power to facilitate academic learning among virtually all of their students. I greatly appreciate McKenzie and Skrla for not only believing this, but helping teachers become better at using that power.

REFERENCE

Hattie, J. A. C. (2009). *Visible learning: A synthesis of 800+ meta-analyses on achievement.* New York: Routledge.

McCarthy, C., Crichlow, W., Dimitriadis, G., & Dolby, N. (Eds.). (2005). *Race, identity, and representation in education* (2nd ed). New York: Routledge.

Sleeter, C. E. (1992). Restructuring schools for multicultural education. *Journal of Teacher Education, 43*(2), 148–156.

Acknowledgments

We first wish to thank the educators—teachers and leaders—in the schools and school districts with whom we work as researchers and professors. What we have learned about equitable and excellent classrooms is grounded in field experiences that were possible only because generous practitioners opened the doors of their schools and classrooms for our research and because our master's and doctoral students teach us as much as we teach them. Particularly, we wish to acknowledge Aldine Independent School District and Superintendent Wanda Bamburg for their ongoing commitment to working in partnership with Texas A&M University to support research on effective classrooms, schools, and districts for highly diverse student populations, as well as all the administrators and teachers in Bryan Independent School District who have helped to generate and refine many of the strategies suggested within this text.

Additionally, we would like to thank the foundations whose financial support enabled us to conduct our research—the Sid W. Richardson Foundation, the William and Flora Hewlett Foundation, and the Houston Endowment. Without the commitment of these foundations to supporting research on school success for children of color and children from low-income homes, our work would not have been possible.

Last, a special thanks to the third member of our creative team, Jim Scheurich, who was not along for this latest adventure because he was immersed in a project of his own, but whose ideas and ongoing friendship remain important parts of everything we produce.

KATHRYN'S ACKNOWLEDGMENTS

Linda, thank you. Working alongside my best friend and traveling buddy, not to mention my daily sounding board and cheerleader, is a gift. Thanks also to my loving and supportive family: Martyn, who is hiking the world with me, all along sipping champagne, gulping coffee, and having great conversations; my children, whom I am so proud of, Kelsey and Kolter McKenzie; my newest family members, Sophie, Andy, Caroline, and Daniel Curtis, who have brought great friendship and joy into my life;

and our newest addition, granddaughter Maddox Kincaid McKenzie, who of course is perfect and gifted. She is also a constant reminder that every child is the manifestation of potential, and developing that potential for goodness depends on all of us and our willingness to care for each child as if that child were our child. And finally, thanks to the other sentient beings that give me a giggle, love me no matter what, and get muddy paw prints all over the furniture, Macy, Nils, and Hank.

LINDA'S ACKNOWLEDGMENTS

I am blessed to work with a colleague who also is my dearest friend; thanks, Kathryn, for everything that you are in my life. Thanks also to Michelle Young and Andrea Rorrer for their friendship and professional expertise that we all share in the midst of incredibly busy lives.

Much love and thanks to my family for their unwavering love and support. My three sons—Steve, Scott, and Eric—are all amazing young men of whom I am incredibly proud. My mom, Mary Jane, and my sister Sandie are strong, smart, and beautiful women who have always believed in me. And my furry family members, Shelby and Drake, provide warmth and love that I could not do without. Thanks also go to the wonderful friends I have made in my "second life" as a serious classic rock and roll fan and Journey aficionada, most especially Debbie and Tom.

PUBLISHER'S ACKNOWLEDGMENTS

Corwin gratefully acknowledges the following individuals for their editorial insight and guidance:

Dano Beal, Gifted/Talented Ed Specialist
Lafayette Elementary School
Seattle Public Schools
Seattle, WA

Rosalind Pijeaux Hale, Professor, Chair, and NCATE Coordinator
Division of Education
Xavier University of Louisiana
New Orleans, LA

Nicky Kemp, Principal
North Callaway R1-Williamsburg Elementary
Williamsburg, MO

Debra K. Las, Science Teacher
John Adams Middle School
Rochester, MN

Betty Brandenburg Yundt, Curriculum Coordinator
Walker Intermediate School
Fort Knox, KY

About the Authors

Kathryn Bell McKenzie is associate professor of educational administration and affiliated faculty member in Women's and Gender Studies at Texas A&M University. Prior to joining the faculty at Texas A&M, Kathryn worked for over 25 years in public education as a classroom teacher, curriculum specialist, assistant principal, principal, and deputy director of the University of Texas/Austin Independent School District Leadership Academy. Maintaining her commitment to practice and practitioners, Kathryn consults and researches extensively in public schools. Her areas of research include equity and social justice in schools, school leadership, and qualitative methodology. Kathryn is associate editor for *Educational Administration Quarterly* and the *International Journal of Qualitative Studies in Education*. She has published extensively in the major journals in her field. Kathryn and her colleagues Linda Skrla and Jim Scheurich are the authors of the bestselling Corwin (2009) book, *Using Equity Audits to Create Equitable and Excellent Schools*.

Linda Skrla is professor of educational administration at Texas A&M University. Prior to joining the Texas A&M faculty in 1997, Linda worked as a middle school and high school teacher and as a campus and district administrator in public schools. Her research focuses on educational equity issues in school leadership, including accountability policy, high-success school districts, and women superintendents. Linda is vice president of Division A of the American Educational Research Association (AERA) and editor of *Educational Administration Quarterly*. She has published extensively in academic journals and has coauthored or coedited five other books, the most recent of which is *Using Equity Audits to Create Equitable and Excellent Schools* (Corwin, 2009).

Introduction

A word as to the education of the heart. We don't believe that this can be imparted through books; it can only be imparted through the loving touch of the teacher.

—Cesar Chavez

It was a Star Trek moment and I was in a parallel universe. I (Kathryn) had just completed a Teaching and Learning Tour, described in detail in Chapter 5, in which I took a group of high school teachers and administrators into several of their colleagues' classrooms as a professional development activity. The goal of this activity was to encourage reflective practice by having teachers and administrators use their colleagues' classrooms as a laboratory to observe instruction, looking for levels of Active Cognitive Engagement, also discussed in Chapter 5. It was not an evaluative activity. The participants were not supposed to judge the quality of the teachers' instruction; we weren't in the classrooms long enough to determine that. The participants were to look specifically at the percentage of students whom they had evidence were actively engaged in thinking about the learning objective. This could be demonstrated in numerous ways, but there needed to be empirical evidence that demonstrated students were thinking about the objective. This evidence could be responses on dry erase boards; it could be group work in which all the students were equally contributing; it could be experiments being conducted in a science lab, and so forth. It could not be students passively sitting as only one or two students raised their hands and offered answers to teacher generated questions.

Prior to this activity, I had discussed with the teachers and administrators the goals of the Teaching and Learning Tours and the concept of Active Cognitive Engagement. I had, also, explicitly explained that this was a professional development activity to enhance personal reflection, not an evaluative activity to judge their colleagues. Each participant was given a reflective guide to complete during the observation. We observed several classrooms, and after each 5- or 10-minute observation, we would go into the hallway and debrief about our observations. One of the questions on the reflective guide was, "What is the percentage of Active Cognitive Engagement?" The participants were asked to actually compute the percentage of students that they had evidence were thinking about the learning objective. In other words, were students engaged in discussion, were they performing an experiment, were they solving problems, were they creating models, and so forth. Nearly all the teachers and administrators who went on the tour indicated high percentages of student engagement. They were aware of the students who were obviously not engaged, the ones who were asleep or doing something completely off task. But, for the most part, they believed the majority of students that were compliant were engaged. However, what I saw was very low levels of engagement. We were in parallel universes. I was having a completely different experience than the others.

I couldn't understand how this was happening. We had discussed the use of the reflective form; I'd explained the purpose of the tour; and I had defined and given examples of Active Cognitive Engagement. How could we see what was going on in the classrooms so differently? They saw students who, for the most part, were well behaved, listening, and responding to the teacher. I saw students sitting in their desks looking at the teacher. I heard a couple of students call out answers to the teachers' questions. I saw teachers answering most of their own questions. But I did not see evidence of high levels of student engagement. I wondered if this is how the teachers participating in the tour experienced their own classroom. Did they look at their students and interpret compliance, sitting and looking at the teacher, as engagement? Did the administrators think this was engagement? Did they think that because one or two students answered a question correctly that everyone in the class was understanding what was being taught? Did they think that when they reviewed the students' algebra homework and worked the problems on the interactive whiteboard and then asked, "Any questions? Do you get this?" that all the students really did "get this"? Did they know at the end of each lesson who did or did not understand what was being taught? It's easy to assume that students are really with us. Often it's not until a formal assessment that we realize some students were not with us. By this time, it is often too late, a gap has opened or grown wider. Moreover, according to national and state assessment data, the students we are not successfully engaging are students of color and those living in poverty.

Back to the Enterprise and the question, "Why couldn't these teachers and administrators see the lack of engagement in the classrooms we were observing?" It seemed so obvious to me. I realized that I was an outsider and not as deeply invested in the relationships with the teachers on this campus. I was far enough removed that when I observed the teachers, I didn't really see myself. These teachers did not represent me. I was no longer a K–12 teacher or administrator, so I no longer felt a strong professional identification with the teachers we were observing as a member of their profession. However, the teachers and administrators seemed to see their colleagues' classrooms and identify with them. They looked for the positive, which addressed the first question on the reflective form—"If this were your classroom, what would you be proud of?" They had much to say about the good things going on in the classroom. However, when it came to the question, "What is the percentage of students that are actively cognitively engaged," they just couldn't see the lack of evidence that students were really thinking about what was being taught. Most students were merely sitting and looking at the teacher, while other students were engaged in discussion with the teacher. Merely observing this compliant behavior was not sufficient to determine how many students were truly engaged. At this point, I realized that if it was difficult for the teachers to see this lack of engagement in other teachers' classrooms, it was probably extremely difficult for them to see it in their own classrooms. As the cliché goes, it's hard to see the forest for the trees.

We continued on with the Teaching and Learning Tours, moving from classroom to classroom and debriefing after each. Most of the teachers and administrators began to see that although they thought students were engaged, they really didn't have any evidence to be certain the students were engaged. I was encouraged, but I worried that although the teachers were beginning to see inequities in the level of engagement in other teachers' classrooms, this might not transfer over into their own. Thinking about my own experience as a K–12 teacher and now as a professor teaching master's and doctoral students, I could attest to the difficulty of ensuring that all students are engaged. I often get on a roll and assume my students are with me. In fact, my experiences working with K–12 schools, auditing for equity, has pushed me to audit my own teaching for equity. In fact, Linda and I try out and incorporate the strategies we suggest within this book in our own university classrooms, and we have had great success improving the engagement level of our students.

At the end of the day, I got in the car and called Linda, as I often do, to share the experience and engage in a little peer debriefing. I explained that at first I was completely baffled when the teachers and administrators didn't see what I had seen—the parallel universe. Then, I was encouraged that as we went into more classrooms, the teachers and administrators began to see the inequity in engagement—that all the students were not engaged, or at least we couldn't determine whether they were engaged or not. I also expressed my concern that, although this had been a good start, I was concerned that the learning might not transfer into the classroom. Moreover, I explained that as the teachers and administrators began to see the inequity in engagement, they wanted to know what the teachers could do to engage the students. They wanted strategies. I told Linda that if we ever wrote another book, it should be one for teachers, one that takes equity audits into the classroom, because that's where the real difference is made for students. Well, several years later, after much more collaboration with teachers and administrators, we have an equity auditing book for teachers. Not everything in this book will work for everyone. Context is paramount. However, we hope that you find an idea or an auditing tool within this book that you can incorporate into your teaching or that will inspire you to create your own tools to ensure that your classroom is equitable and excellent.

A BRIEF OVERVIEW OF OUR WORK ON EQUITY AUDITS

We, along with our colleague Jim Scheurich, have been working for over a decade to employ equity audits as a tool for improving schools and school districts. Jim and Linda, along with Juanita Garcia and Glen Nolly, introduced the concept of equity auditing in schools in their article "Equity Audits: A Practical Leadership Tool for Developing Equitable and Excellent Schools" in *Educational Administration Quarterly* (2004). This article generated an enormous amount of interest in equity audits, so much so that a chapter was dedicated to equity audits in Jim and Linda's first book for Corwin, *Leadership for Equity and Excellence Creating High-Achievement Classrooms, Schools, and Districts* (2003).

One chapter, though, was not enough. District and school leaders, along with professors in educational leadership programs, wanted more specific and practical applications of equity audits. This interest lead to the second book on equity audits, *Using Equity Audits to Create Equitable and Excellent Schools*. By this time, I was a professor, having left public education, where I had worked as a teacher and principal for over 25 years. I joined Linda and Jim as a coauthor of the second book. This second book met with great success, and we began to use equity audits in our work with schools and school districts throughout the nation and beyond. Although this work was helping to improve schools and school districts, it was not specifically meeting the needs of individual teachers. This, the third book in the series, directly addresses auditing for equity and excellence in the classroom. To help the reader who may not have read the previous books, all of these books are based on the concept that high-quality teaching combined with programmatic equity leads to academic achievement equity. (See Figure 4.3 in Chapter 4 for a graphic representation of this concept.)

To further explain, we define a high-quality teacher as one who has an equity consciousness and excellent teaching skills (see chapters 2 and 3). Programs, which we define broadly, such as special education and even discipline, are equitable when there is not a disproportionate number of students from any population group represented within a program (see chapters 5–8). For example, if 30% of a school population is white students, white students should not compose 60% of the gifted and talented students. This is a disproportionate number of students from one population group represented within the gifted and talented program. Last, we consider equity in academic achievement to have been attained when all students, regardless of race, gender, economic level, and so forth, achieve at high levels. In other words, there is no achievement gap.

PREVIEWS OF CHAPTERS 2–9

The chapters in this book are divided into two sections. The first section (chapters 2–4) focuses on the conceptual and historical framework for this work. This section lays out our explanation of equitable and excellent teaching, including equity consciousness and high-quality teaching skills, as well as the history of equity audits that led to our use of this tool to improve school districts, schools, and classrooms. The second section (chapters 5–9) concentrates on specific areas to address when auditing within the classroom for equity and excellence. In this section we provide specific strategies for teachers to use to ensure that they are teaching well all of their students. A brief preview of the content of each chapter follows.

Section I: Conceptual and Historical Frameworks

Chapter 2

In this chapter, we introduce the two aspects of equitable and excellent teaching that research (both our own and a considerable body of work conducted by other scholars) has consistently identified as important factors in classrooms and schools that are successful with diverse students. These two aspects are *equity consciousness* and *high-quality teaching skills.*

Chapter 3

Chapter 3 focuses on the qualities of an equitable and excellent classroom. Although this chapter is about the classroom, we include an example of an equitable and excellent school to demonstrate what can happen when classroom instruction meets the needs of all students. Included is a Classroom Equity Assessment you can use to determine the level of equity within your classroom.

Chapter 4

This chapter concludes Section I by offering a historical look at equity audits. Included are equity audits in international settings and equity audits in U.S. education. In regard to U.S. education, we discuss civil rights auditing, curriculum audits, and accountability audits. We conclude this chapter by explaining the equity audit tool and the ways we have used this in schools.

Section II: Equity Auditing in the Classroom

Chapter 5

We begin the second section, which covers auditing in the classroom, by discussing auditing for teaching and learning. We begin by briefly reviewing the research on teaching and learning and then introduce the concepts of *Active Cognitive Engagement* and *Zone of Self-Efficacy*. We believe for students to learn they must be actively cognitively engaged and be in the teacher's Zone of Self-Efficacy. Additionally, we offer an equity tool—Teaching and Learning Tour—that we find useful both in determining the level of Active Cognitive Engagement in a classroom and identifying which students are in or out of the Zone of Self-Efficacy.

Chapter 6

In this chapter, we discuss auditing for discipline. We begin with a review of the research on discipline disproportionality, that is, the extent to which students in a given subgroup may be subject to behavioral discipline more often than students in other subgroups. This is followed by examples of discipline disproportionality. We conclude by providing three tools to audit your classroom disciplinary practices. These include a reflective survey, a discipline record, and a family communication chart.

Chapter 7

Next we examine auditing for parental involvement. Again, we start with the review of the literature, focusing now on parental or family involvement. Then, we address in more detail the six broad categories of findings in this research. These include a sense of welcome, misconceptions among stakeholders, use of and issues related to resources, home context and student performance, program structures, and roles of those involved in school-family connections. We conclude by offering a Classroom Parental Involvement Inventory to assist you in auditing for parental involvement.

Chapter 8

The last auditing category we address is programmatic equity. In this chapter we provide examples of the types of programs that should be audited and strategies that can be used to audit these programs. The programs we chose to address include advanced placement, gifted and talented, and special education. We provide a literature review that addresses issues of inequity in each of these programs followed by examples that illustrate these inequities. As we did in the other chapters in this section, we offer an auditing tool to address equity in each of the three programs we focus on.

Chapter 9

In our concluding chapter we pull all the pieces together by reviewing and summarizing each of the main concepts we have addressed.

CHAPTER CONCLUSION

Whereas our previous work has focused on district- and school-level audits, the goal of this book is to take audits to the classroom. We believe teachers are the ones who most impact student learning. Moreover, we understand that you cannot have equitable and excellent districts or schools unless there are equitable and excellent classrooms. We believe the auditing tools we offer in this text can provide teachers with usable classroom strategies to improve excellence and equity, which will improve schools, school districts, and education in general in the United States. It's time all our students have the quality education they deserve.

Section I

Conceptual and Historical Frameworks

2 Equitable and Excellent Teaching

The dream begins with a teacher who believes in you, who tugs and pushes and leads you to the next plateau.

—Dan Rather

In our earlier work (McKenzie, Skrla, & Scheurich, 2006; Skrla, McKenzie, & Scheurich, 2009), we discussed two aspects of Equitable and Excellent Teaching (EET) that research (both our own and a considerable body of work conducted by other scholars) has consistently identified as critical for teachers to be successful with all students. These two aspects are equity consciousness and high-quality teaching skills (see Figure 2.1).

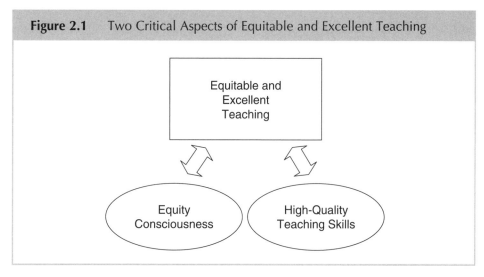

Figure 2.1 Two Critical Aspects of Equitable and Excellent Teaching

In this chapter, we expand our discussion of equity consciousness and high-quality teaching skills and link these more specifically to individual teachers and their classrooms. We turn first to equity consciousness.

EQUITY CONSCIOUSNESS PREASSESSMENT

To begin our discussion of equity consciousness, we have developed a short preassessment for you to use to gauge your current level of equity consciousness (see Figure 2.2 on page 20 at the end of this chapter). Since this is a pretest, it appears before any further discussion of the concept so that readers can use it as a benchmark to see where they are in relation to equity consciousness as we have conceptualized it.

Additional discussion of the rationale for each item on this preassessment and the research on which these are based follows in the next sections.

EQUITY CONSCIOUSNESS DEFINED

The term *equity consciousness* appears regularly in the field of education as well as in other fields of scholarship and practice. Equity consciousness as a concept can be found in widely diverse places, including discussions of U.S. Supreme Court decisions affecting educational equity (Kirp, 1995, p. 107), education policy documents in international settings (e.g., the *Gender Equity Education Act* passed by the government of Taiwan in 2004), and research literature on ethics in conducting ethnographic (field-based, qualitative) research (Laiore, 2003).

The term *equity consciousness* in all these settings generally means a person's awareness of the level of equity and inequity present in behaviors, policies, settings, organizations, and outcomes. In other words, equity consciousness refers to how *aware* or *mindful* people are as to whether others around them are receiving fair and equitable treatment, how well they understand the phenomenon of inequity, and how willing they are to become involved in solutions.

In our discussion of equity consciousness, however, both here and in our earlier work, we mean something quite specific—a set of four beliefs based on our own and others' research in schools and districts that have demonstrated substantial, sustained progress in raising achievement for all students and in closing achievement gaps among students in differing racial and socioeconomic (SES) groups. These four beliefs are

   1. that all children (except only a very small percentage, e.g., those with profound disabilities) are capable of high levels of academic success;

2. that *all* children means *all*, regardless of a child's race, social class, gender, sexual orientation, learning difference, culture, language, religion, and so on;

3. that the adults in school are primarily responsible for student learning; and

4. that traditional school practices may work for some students but are not working for *all* children. Therefore, if we are going to eliminate the achievement gap, it requires a change in our practices. (Skrla et al., 2009, pp. 82–83)

RESEARCH ON EQUITY CONSCIOUSNESS

Many people might read the above list of the four central beliefs that compose our view of equity consciousness and think, "Well, *of course* everyone in public schools believes those things." The same people might wonder why it is even necessary to have a discussion about the topic, much less devote an entire chapter to it. It seems intuitive that the people who chose to work with children and young adults in schools would believe wholeheartedly and enthusiastically in students' capacity for academic success and in adults' responsibility for seeing that that capacity becomes reality.

Research on this issue, however, shows that, despite how intuitive it might seem that everyone in schools believes in all children's capability to be highly academically successful, the real-life views held by educators often are much different. Consider, for example, these findings from the 2009 *MetLife Survey of the American Teacher:*

- Nearly nine in ten teachers (86%) and principals (89%) believe that setting high expectations for all students would have a major impact on improving student achievement.
- Most teachers (84%) are very confident that they have the knowledge and skills necessary to enable all of their students to succeed academically.

[YET]
- Only 36% of teachers and 51% of principals believe that all of their students have the ability to succeed academically. (MetLife, 2009, p. 3)

Thus, even though the overwhelming majority of teachers believe that high expectations are important for improving student achievement, and even though most believe they have the necessary teaching skills, *only about a third of teachers* believe that all of their students actually have the ability to succeed. This is a discouraging finding given what we know from research about how holding high expectations for the success of all students translates into actual classroom practices that are important influences on how much students learn (Edmonds, 1979). This is the reason we emphasize, in our first component of equity consciousness, a belief that all students can learn at high academic levels.

Furthermore, teachers' beliefs about students' abilities to be highly academically successful tend to be unevenly distributed based on students' race and family income status. Research has shown that, in general, teachers have less positive views of the capability of African American and Latino/a students (as compared to their white and Asian American peers) and believe students from low-income homes to be, as a group, less academically capable. As Diamond, Randolph, and Spillane (2004) found,

> Our data showed that teachers' beliefs about students were patterned by the race and social class composition of the student population. . . . When students were majority African American and low-income, teachers held more deficit-oriented beliefs about them than when students were majority white or Chinese, or when a higher percentage came from middle-income families. Our data further demonstrate that teachers' sense of responsibility for student learning was higher in contexts where they saw students as possessing greater learning resources. When students' deficits were emphasized, teachers believed that students' lack of motivation, families, and limited skills undermined teachers' ability to effectively teach. (p. 93)

This pattern of unevenly distributed belief in students' ability to be highly academically successful is the reason for our emphasis on the second component of our conceptualization of equity consciousness—that *all* means *literally all* students.

The findings of Diamond et al. (2004) also point to the importance of the third component of our idea of equity consciousness—the responsibility of the adults in schools for ensuring academic success. Research suggests that teachers, when asked about the causes of persistent achievement gaps among student groups in public schools, overwhelmingly cite factors *external* to the schools and out of the direct control of educators. For example, a recent survey of North Carolina teachers found that

> secondary mathematics teachers endorsed various explanations for the achievement gap; our results suggest that the most frequently

endorsed factors were related to student characteristics. . . . In particular, differences in students' motivational levels, work ethic, and family or parent support were cited. (Bol & Berry, 2005, p. 40)

There is little question that factors such as student motivation and family support do matter, but to rely solely on these factors as explanations for why achievement gaps persist is to avoid accepting responsibility for the *other* important factors that also contribute to the gap that are *within* the power of educators to control and change. Education Trust's Katie Haycock explained it this way:

When we speak with adults, no matter where we are in the country, they make the same comments. "They're too poor." "Their parents don't care." "They come to school without an adequate breakfast." "They don't have enough books in the home." "Indeed, there aren't enough parents in the home." Their reasons, in other words, are always about the children and their families.

Young people, however, have different answers. They talk about teachers who often do not know the subjects that they are teaching. They talk about counselors who consistently underestimate their potential and place them in lower-level courses. They talk about principals who dismiss their concerns. And they talk about a curriculum and a set of expectations that feel so miserably low-level that they literally bore the students right out the school door.

When we ask, "What about the things that the adults are always talking about—neighborhood violence, single-parent homes, and so on?"—the young people's responses are fascinating. "Sure, those things matter," they say. "But what hurts us more is that you teach us less."

The truth is that the data bear out what the young people are saying. It's not that issues like poverty and parental education don't matter. Clearly they do. But we take the students who have less to begin with and then systematically give them less in school. In fact, we give these students less of everything that we believe makes a difference. We do this in hundreds of different ways. (Haycock, 2001, pp. 7–8)

The point Haycock makes underscores the importance of the fourth component of our concept of equity consciousness—educators' acceptance of the inequity built into traditional practices and routines of schooling and acknowledgment that these must change if achievement gaps are to close and if all students are to achieve high academic success.

As our colleagues who study Total Quality Management (TQM) often point out, *every system is ideally designed to produce what it is currently producing.* In other words, whatever systems and routines are currently in place in your classroom are ideally suited to continue to produce what you currently are getting—in terms of student achievement, discipline, and so forth. If you want things in your classroom to change significantly for the better, you will have to be open to making significant changes to what goes on in that classroom. However, not only will you need to consider your equity consciousness, the first aspect of equitable and excellent teaching, you will also need to examine your teaching skills, the second aspect of EET.

RESEARCH ON HIGH-QUALITY TEACHING SKILLS

The research findings on teaching that is successful with all students are consistent, although the language used by the various researchers may not be exactly the same. Figure 2.3 summarizes the research-based recommendations for high-quality teaching skills provided by selected renowned researchers who have studied teaching in schools serving diverse learners.

Figure 2.3	Research-Based Recommendations for High-Quality Teaching Skills	
Delpit (2006)	*Ladson-Billings (1995)*	*Sleeter (2008)*
See students' brilliance: Do not teach less content to poor, urban children but instead, teach more!	Believe that students are capable of academic success.	Hold high expectation for students' learning, regardless of how they are doing now.
Ensure that all students gain access to "basic skills"—the conventions and strategies that are essential to success in American society.	See pedagogy as art—unpredictable, always in the process of becoming.	Engage students academically by building on what they know and what interests them.
Demand critical thinking, whatever methodology or instructional program is used.	See yourself as a member of your students' community.	Relate to students' families and communities, and read them in culturally accurate ways.
Provide the emotional ego strength to challenge racist societal views of the competence and worthiness of the children and their families.	See teaching as a way to give back to the community.	Envision students as constructive participants in a multicultural democracy.

Figure 2.3 (*continued*)

Recognize and build on children's strengths.	Believe in a Freirean notion of "teaching as mining" (1974, p. 76) or pulling knowledge out.	
Use familiar metaphors, analogies, and experiences from the children's world to connect what children already know to school knowledge.	Maintain fluid teacher-student relationships.	
Create a sense of family and caring in the service of academic achievement.	Demonstrate connectedness with all of the students.	
Monitor and assess children's needs, and then address them with a wealth of diverse strategies.	Develop a community of learners.	
Honor and respect the children's home culture.	Encourage students to learn collaboratively and be responsible for another.	
Foster a sense of children's connection to community—to something greater than themselves.	Believe knowledge is not static; it is shared, recycled, and constructed.	
	Believe knowledge must be viewed critically.	
	Be passionate about knowledge and learning.	
	Scaffold, or build bridges, to facilitate learning.	
	Believe and ensure that assessment must be multifaceted, incorporating multiple forms of excellence.	

Consistent with the work of the selected authors above, our previous work on this topic (McKenzie & Lozano, 2008; McKenzie & Scheurich, 2004; McKenzie et al., 2006; Skrla et al., 2009) positions the teacher as the most important factor in ensuring equitable and excellent classrooms. In our 2009 Corwin book, *Using Equity Audits to Create Equitable and Excellent Schools,* we identified and provided an extended discussion of nine skills that we think are among the most important for all teachers to possess. These skills are

- using consistent and reliable classroom procedures and routines;
- clearly communicating expectations for learning;

- stimulating students with high-level and complex tasks;
- ensuring students are actively, cognitively engaged;
- extending student learning through teacher-to-student and student-to-student discussion;
- frequently assessing individual student learning;
- differentiating instruction to meet individual student needs and capitalize on individual assets;
- using an asset model to respond to students' varying cultures; and
- demonstrating respect and care in all interactions with all students and students' families. (Skrla et al., pp. 90–96)

Now that you know what constitutes high-quality teaching skills, you will need to assess your own teaching. We will assist you with this in the following chapters, where we provide you with self-assessments and strategies for improving both your teaching skills and equity consciousness.

CHAPTER CONCLUSION

In this chapter we discussed our framework for Equitable and Excellent Teaching (EET), including equity consciousness and high-quality teaching skills. We began with a preassessment to aid you in determining your level of equity consciousness and followed this with a definition and discussion of equity consciousness and related research. Next, we introduced the second aspect of EET, high-quality teaching skills, offering discussion and research from renowned scholars in the field of teaching excellence and equity. The important takeaway point from this chapter is that teachers must know how to teach; that is, they must have high-quality teaching skills. However, to be an equitable and excellent teacher, they also have to believe that all their students can learn at high levels and ensure that their students do; that is, they must have an equity consciousness. Stated another way, a teacher who has good teaching skills but is only teaching some of the students in the class is not an equitable and excellent teacher. EET teachers believe all students can learn at high levels and that it is their responsibility to teach to all students. They have high-quality teaching skills *and* an equity consciousness. In the next chapter, we describe equitable and excellent classrooms and provide a look into a school where teachers and administrators are working consistently to ensure equity and excellence.

DISCUSSION QUESTIONS AND ACTIVITIES

1. Download the complete *Met Life Survey of the American Teacher,* http://www.metlife.com/assets/cao/contributions/foundation/

american-teacher/MetLife_Teacher_Survey_2009.pdf. Which findings from this survey affirm what you would have predicted to be true? Which are surprising to you?

2. Extraordinary teachers who transform students' lives through the power of high expectations have been a frequent focus for Hollywood films, such as *Stand and Deliver, Dead Poets Society, Dangerous Minds, Mr. Holland's Opus,* and *To Sir With Love.* Why do you think this type of transformative teaching is often limited to a few exceptional individuals and is not standard practice for many or most teachers in schools?

3. Reflect on the teachers and professors you have had in your own schooling experiences thus far. Can you think of particular individuals who communicated to you that they believed you were capable of being successful with the subject/material they taught, even when you yourself might have doubted that you could learn it? If so, what effect did this have on you? In what ways did these teachers let you know that they believed you could be successful? Conversely, have you had teachers in the past who you sensed did not believe you could learn what was being taught in their classes? If so, how did this affect you? In what ways was this lack of belief in your ability to learn communicated?

Figure 2.2   Equity Consciousness Preassessment

For the 10 items below, circle the number that represents your level of agreement with each statement based on the scale provided, with 1 being "strongly disagree," and 5 being "strongly agree." In responding to these statements, we encourage you to be as thoughtful and honest as possible about what you *really believe*.

1 = strongly disagree
2 = disagree
3 = neither disagree nor agree
4 = agree
5 = strongly agree

1. All the students in my classroom are capable of mastering the curriculum and achieving academic success.

    1   2   3   4   5

2. All my students, regardless of their life circumstances, bring intellectual, cultural, and personal assets with them to my classroom that I can build on through my teaching.

    1   2   3   4   5

3. I see the race, social class, gender, sexual orientation, language, learning differences, culture, and religion of my students as important parts of their identities (i.e., who these students are).

    1   2   3   4   5

4. Open acknowledgment and discussion of racism, classism, sexism, and other forms of discrimination present in my school can be a useful step toward advancing equity.

    1   2   3   4   5

5. The responsibility for student learning in my classroom lies primarily with me and with the other adults in my school.

    1   2   3   4   5

6. Most parents care deeply about their children's learning and want them to do well in school.

    1   2   3   4   5

7. The regular routines and procedures in my school do not serve some students and student groups as well as they serve other students and student groups.

    1   2   3   4   5

8. If I do everything the same way this school year as I did it last year, it is highly likely that the results (in terms of student learning) will be the same.

    1   2   3   4   5

9. As a classroom teacher, there is much I can do to change inequitable procedures and practices.

    1   2   3   4   5

10. If I attempt to change the status quo in my classroom and implement more equity-conscious strategies, my fellow teachers and other colleagues may not celebrate and support my efforts.

    1   2   3   4   5

Add your scores for each of the ten items and use the scale below to see where your current level of equity consciousness falls according to our definition of the concept.

45–50	Indicates highly developed equity consciousness
40–44	Indicates well-developed equity consciousness
35–39	Indicates somewhat developed equity consciousness
34 or below	Indicates minimally developed equity consciousness

3 Qualities of Equitable and Excellent Classrooms

Good schools, like good societies and good families, celebrate and cherish diversity.

—Deborah Meier

Classrooms that are equitable and excellent are ones in which all students, regardless of factors external to the classroom such as race, ethnicity, culture, gender, learning differences, economic level, and so forth, are respected, and students are provided the instructional support necessary for them to be successful. This, though, is not always easy and, with the pressures of high stakes accountability, it can seem almost impossible. Nonetheless, there are models of success. For example, Tice Elementary School in Galena Park, Texas, has high academic achievement for nearly all students. Currently, according to the Texas Education Agency (2009), Tice has over 600 students—approximately 35% are African American[1], 61% are Hispanic, and 3% are white. Moreover, 86% are labeled Economically Disadvantaged and 24% are labeled Limited English Proficient. The racial/ethnic composition of the current teaching staff at Tice is 34% African American, 13% Hispanic, 51% white, and 2% Asian. The average years of teaching experience is 13 years.

AN EXAMPLE OF AN EQUITABLE AND EXCELLENT SCHOOL: TICE ELEMENTARY

We became familiar with Tice during a 2004–2006 Hewlett-funded study of successful school districts that serve diverse, predominantly low-income

21

students (Skrla, McKenzie, Scheurich, & Dickerson, 2007). As part of that study, we observed classrooms at Tice and interviewed the principal, dean of instruction, and teachers. At the time of that research, Tice was one of the highest-performing elementary schools in Texas, based on state accountability tests. Since that time Tice has only become better.

In 2009, 98% of Tice's students met state passing standards on all tests (reading, writing, math, and science) in grades 3–5. Moreover, it was honored with the Gold Performance Rating (the highest given by the state) for commended performance in all tested areas. This means that a significant percentage of the students taking the test scored at high levels, levels above those required to meet expectations. Overall, on a four-category scale, which includes the categories *academically unacceptable, acceptable, recognized,* and *exemplary,* Tice received the highest rating, "exemplary." This means Tice, a racially, linguistically, and culturally diverse school that serves large numbers of students who are designated Economically Disadvantaged, scored at levels comparable to those of the wealthiest schools in the state.

One might think that Tice achieved these levels of success through extraordinary teaching or increased resources. But that is not the case. In fact, the teaching, as we observed, was basic. However, every teacher in every classroom was teaching every student for most of the class time. No student was "out of the zone." (See Chapter 5 for an explanation of "the zone.") That is, no student was left on her or his own to learn. Each and every student had a caring teacher who insisted and ensured that the student learn at high levels.

Initially, this required getting students "on grade level," since many of the students were performing "below grade level." In other words, teachers had to instruct students in the requisite skills they needed to be able to do on–grade level work. This was not just left to the classroom teacher. The principal removed four master teachers[2] from regular classroom teaching responsibilities—they no longer had classroom teaching assignments—and assigned them to teach the students with the greatest needs. This was done by pulling the lowest-performing five students, in math and reading, out of each teacher's class and having the master teachers provide these students with intensive instruction in the requisite skills for one hour per day. This was not done during the regular math and reading instruction time in the student's classroom. It did not replace the regular classroom teacher's instruction; it added to it. Thus, these students received additional support in math and reading in an effort to get them to grade level. Additionally, it was not always the same five students receiving the intensive instructional support. Tice used frequent school-wide benchmark tests to measure student progress toward curriculum mastery and used these test results to target which students needed help with which skills.

At the same time, the principal and dean of instruction began working with teachers at each grade level every day, aligning curriculum and developing lessons and assessments. We realize this sounds remarkable—that a principal and dean of instruction would spend the majority of their day, every day, working on teaching and instruction with teachers. However, that is what they did, and it paid off.[3] Eventually, through the efforts of the master teachers and the concerted efforts of the principal, dean of instruction, and teachers, nearly all students began performing on grade level. This literally closed the achievement gaps and made everyone's job easier. The classroom teachers could focus on the curriculum for just their grade levels instead of trying to teach a large percentage of students who were one or more grade levels behind. This eliminated the need to differentiate at extreme levels. The teachers still differentiated instruction, but now they could differentiate to take students further, not differentiate to make up for gaps.

In summary, we are saying that at the classroom level or even the school level, one can teach all students well without doing anything extraordinary. Equity and excellence can be achieved if each and every teacher commits to and then ensures that each student is taught all day every day. That doesn't sound too hard, but it is. Teaching those students who we find easy to teach is not hard. But teaching students who we find difficult to teach, for an array of reasons, is tough. However, as Tice demonstrated, it can be done. It requires, though, that we transform our classrooms into equitable communities. To do this, we first have to determine the level of equity in our classrooms.

CLASSROOM EQUITY ASSESSMENT

To assist you in determining the level of equity you currently have in your classroom, we offer the following assessment (see Figure 3.1 on page 27 at the end of this chapter).

Now that you have established the level of equity in your classroom, if you scored at the "strong efforts" level, you may be feeling exhilarated, knowing that you have, indeed, ensured high levels of equity in your classroom. If you scored at the "moderate efforts" level, you may be feeling somewhat discouraged that, although you have moderate levels of equity in your classroom, there is need for improvement. And, if you scored at the "insignificant efforts" level, you may be feeling defeated, wondering how you can possible do everything that would be needed to ensure that all students are successful. You may even be feeling angry—angry that the expectation is too high or the work too much. You may believe that you are working extremely hard to reach and teach all your students, but that some students just aren't trying hard enough, don't have the skills to be successful, or have parents who don't seem to be working as hard as you to ensure their child's school success.

We know that most teachers work tremendously hard. In fact, in the decades that we have worked as school teachers and administrators and now as researchers and consultants in schools, we have found that most teachers work extremely hard, even those that are not meeting with high levels of student success. One might ask, "Why are teachers who are working hard not having high levels of success?" To answer this, we return to our research at Tice Elementary. The teachers at Tice aren't necessarily working harder; rather, they have learned what to pay attention to and where to put their efforts. To illustrate, at the time we were conducting research at Tice, the principal required all the teachers to leave the campus at 3:45, a mere 30 minutes after the students left. As the principal explained to us, he wanted the teachers working hard for the time they were at school, but then he wanted them to go home and take care of their personal lives so that they could give their full attention and efforts to their students when they were at school. He understood that to be productive, people need to be able to focus on their work. He also understood that people need time to be away from work, mentally and physically, so they can recharge.

This may seem contrary to what you have experienced in your school. Many of the schools we work with seem to be trying to squeeze out more and more of everyone, every minute, of every day. This is an honest attempt to work harder and harder to try to catch up and close the gaps. However, much of this work, as well meaning as it is, is not productive or may even be counterproductive. So, what are schools like Tice—that are not exhausting everyone, yet are being highly successful—doing to accomplish this? In the subsequent chapters, we hope to provide you with answers to this question.

CHAPTER CONCLUSION

In this chapter we offered research on equitable and excellent classrooms and gave you a look into a school, Tice Elementary, where there is both equity and excellence. Moreover, we explained that to achieve the level of success that Tice Elementary accomplished does not require extraordinary teaching. It does, however, require that the teachers in every classroom teach every student well. This sounds so simple, but as you know, it is not always easy to do. To help you, we provided the Classroom Equity Assessment so you can determine the level of equity in your classroom so you have a starting point.

Furthermore, now that you have an understanding of teacher quality, including equity consciousness and high-quality teaching skills, we will move on to an explanation of equity audits and how you can use these in your classroom to determine the level of equity in teaching and learning, discipline, parental involvement, and programs such as advanced placement, gifted and talented, and special education. We begin the discussion on auditing in the next chapter with a historical overview of auditing in general, and auditing in education specifically.

DISCUSSION QUESTIONS AND ACTIVITIES

1. For an extended exploration of the characteristics of classrooms that are equitable and excellent and moving profiles of the teachers in such classrooms, read Gloria Ladson-Billings's (1994) award-winning book *The Dreamkeepers: Successful Teachers of African American Children.*

2. Do you currently work in or have you ever worked in or visited a campus that was having high academic success serving a highly diverse population of students such as that described in our profile of Tice Elementary? If so, what similarities do you see between the Tice story and what you've experienced? If not, how might you identify such a campus and arrange time to visit it, either on your own or with a group of colleagues?

NOTES

1. The labels used herein that refer to racial, ethnic, economic, and instructional categories, such as Special Education and Limited English Proficient, are the terms used by the Texas Education Agency rather than terms chosen and preferred by the authors.

2. It's important to explain that at Tice, "master teacher" really meant master teacher. These teachers had a demonstrated record of high student success. These were not political appointments. The teachers were chosen because of the exceptional quality of their teaching.

3. At this point you are probably questioning how the principal and dean could have the time to do this with disciplinary issues, parent issues, and so forth. This is the point. They put their attention on what was most important, instruction. However, they did have to set up structures for attending to the daily management of the school, which they did. We won't expand on these here, but we will demonstrate in the following chapters how each teacher addressed many of the issues, which we refer to as microdiversions (McKenzie & Lozano, 2008), that prevent those in school from focusing intently on instruction. The point is that disciplinary issues, parental issues, and so forth are the responsibility of everyone

in a school. When they are addressed at the classroom level, but this means in every classroom, they don't end up in the principal's office. This leaves the principal and others available to actively work with and support teachers, resulting in support for students. In the following chapters, we provide strategies for being preemptive so that concerns like discipline and parental issues don't become "issues" at all.

Figure 3.1   Classroom Equity Assessment

Directions: Consider all population groups represented in your class. These might include groups designated by race, gender, economic class, learning difference, ethnicity, culture, home language, and so forth. Using the following scale, circle the number that indicates the frequency at which you perform the stated actions. Once you have assigned a number to each statement, add all the numbers to get your total score. This will give you an indication of the level of equity within your classroom.

    5 = always
    4 = frequently
    3 = sometimes
    2 = seldom
    1 = never

In my class,

1. I discipline students as often and at the same level of severity, regardless of their race, gender, economic class, and so forth.
       1   2   3   4   5
2. I ensure that students have equal access to my attention, regardless of their race, gender, economic class, and so forth.
       1   2   3   4   5
3. I give enough instructional support for students to master the learning objectives being taught, regardless of their race, gender, economic class, and so forth.
       1   2   3   4   5
4. I am aware of every student's instructional level and differentiate instruction to meet student needs, regardless of their race, gender, economic class, and so forth.
       1   2   3   4   5
5. I know each student's achievement level in my class and on district, state, and national achievement tests, regardless of their race, gender, economic class, and so forth.
       1   2   3   4   5
6. My instruction draws from and builds on students' backgrounds, regardless of their race, gender, economic class, and so forth.
       1   2   3   4   5
7. I look for learning differences in students and refer them for gifted or advanced education and/or special education, regardless of their race, gender, economic class, and so forth.
       1   2   3   4   5
8. I develop partnerships with students' families, regardless of their race, gender, economic class, and so forth.
       1   2   3   4   5
9. I provide a rigorous curriculum and challenging instruction to students, regardless of their race, gender, economic class, and so forth.
       1   2   3   4   5
10. I am respectful and develop relationships with students, regardless of their race, gender, economic class, and so forth.
       1   2   3   4   5

Add your scores for each of the ten items and use the scale below to see where your current level of equity consciousness falls according to our definition of the concept.

45–50	Indicates strong efforts to ensure equity
39–44	Indicates moderate efforts to ensure equity
Below 34	Indicates insignificant efforts to ensure equity

4 Auditing for Equity and Excellence

Data! Data! Data! . . . I can't make bricks without clay.
—Sherlock Holmes

Experts often possess more data than judgment.
—Colin Powell

In this chapter, we provide a brief history and background for the concept of equity audits. This chapter is included to frame the context for our discussion of the classroom-level equity audits that are the focus of this book. We have used the concept of equity audits in our two previous books for Corwin Press, but equity audits are not something we originated. The terminology has been and continues to be used frequently in the United States and in international settings in a variety of contexts, including education. We have written this chapter for readers who are interested in learning about the history, evolution, and applications of the concept of equity auditing as we are using it. We first explore broader uses of the term and then turn to a more detailed discussion of equity audits in U.S. education.

EQUITY AUDITS IN INTERNATIONAL SETTINGS

An Internet search for the term *equity audits* will produce references to equity audits (also known as *representivity* audits) in a variety of international arenas in both the private and public sectors. Businesses, industries, and organizations are commonly required by governments and regulatory agencies around the globe to conduct (or conduct voluntarily) equity audits focused on a range of issues, including gender equity, pay equity, equitable access to health care, technology equity, and other forms of equity.

To illustrate one form that international equity audits take, the National Health Service (NHS) office located in Bristol, UK, advocates the use of health equity audits. The NHS Bristol definition of health equity audits found on their website highlights the purpose and process of these equity audits:

A health equity audit (HEA) is the process by which local partners:

- Systematically review inequities in the causes of ill health and in access to effective services and their outcomes for a defined population.
- Ensure that action required is agreed and incorporated into local plans, services, and practice.
- Evaluate the impact of the actions on reducing inequity.

It provides an opportunity for statutory agencies and Local Strategic Partnerships to develop common understandings of their local health inequalities and to ensure that resources are allocated to tackle them. (NHS Bristol, n.d.)

Thus, for health care agencies and community partners in the service area of this division of the UK NHS, health equity audits are a recommended strategy to identify and systematically address gaps in and differential access to health care.

Another international example of the concept of equity audits in use is the government of Western Australia's (WA) advocacy for conducting pay equity audits to identify and address gender inequities in pay systems. The WA government website provides a toolkit that is "a resource package for organisations to use in turning data from a pay equity audit into achievable pay equity strategies" (Government of Western Australia, 2009). As with the UK health equity audit example, the emphasis of the WA pay equity audit process is both on *identifying* patterns of inequity and on *implementing* strategies to address them.

These examples of the different forms equity audits can take in the United Kingdom and Australia are just two among many that can be found, all of which illustrate the basic concept of equity auditing; that is, data are gathered and analyzed to reveal patterns of equity and inequity in specific focus areas, and strategies are formulated and implemented to address inequities revealed by the data analysis.

EQUITY AUDITS IN U.S. EDUCATION

As with equity audits conducted in international government, business, and education arenas, equity auditing in U.S. education developed as a process based on the use of data to reveal areas of equity and inequity and to plan for improvement. Furthermore, the idea of equity auditing in U.S. education has historical roots in at least three different areas. Equity audits have been used in (1) civil rights enforcement, (2) curriculum auditing and math/science reform, and (3) state accountability.

Civil Rights Enforcement

One historical precedent for our conceptualization of equity audits can be found in the extensive compliance review process conducted by the U.S. Department of Education Office for Civil Rights (OCR). OCR is charged with enforcing federal antidiscrimination laws in public schools. According to its website,

> The Office for Civil Rights enforces several Federal civil rights laws that prohibit discrimination in programs or activities that receive federal financial assistance from the Department of Education. Discrimination on the basis of race, color, and national origin is prohibited by Title VI of the Civil Rights Act of 1964; sex discrimination is prohibited by Title IX of the Education Amendments of 1972; discrimination on the basis of disability is prohibited by Section 504 of the Rehabilitation Act of 1973; and age discrimination is prohibited by the Age Discrimination Act of 1975. These civil rights laws enforced by OCR extend to all state education agencies, elementary and secondary school systems, colleges and universities, vocational schools, proprietary schools, state vocational rehabilitation agencies, libraries, and museums that receive U.S. Department of Education funds. Areas covered may include, but are not limited to: admissions, recruitment, financial aid, academic programs, student treatment and services, counseling and guidance, discipline, classroom assignment, grading, vocational education, recreation, physical education, athletics, housing, and employment. OCR also has responsibilities under Title II of the Americans with Disabilities Act of 1990 (prohibiting disability discrimination by public entities, whether or not they receive federal financial assistance). In addition, as of January 8, 2002, OCR enforces the Boy Scouts of America Equal Access Act (Section 9525 of the Elementary and Secondary Education Act of 1965, as amended by the No Child Left Behind Act of 2001). Under the Boy Scouts of America Equal Access Act, no public elementary school or state or local education agency that provides an opportunity for one or more outside youth or community groups to meet on school premises or in school facilities before

or after school hours shall deny equal access or a fair opportunity to meet to, or discriminate against, any group officially affiliated with the Boy Scouts of America, or any other youth group listed in Title 36 of the United States Code as a patriotic society. (U.S. Department of Education, n.d.)

Thus, OCR has broad responsibility for enforcement of numerous federal laws designed to prevent discrimination in public agencies, including public schools.

As part of this enforcement mission, OCR investigates complaints and conducts a limited number of extensive compliance reviews. For fiscal year 2008, OCR received 6,194 complaints, the majority of which fell into two categories: 51% involved disability discrimination, and 16% were related to discrimination based on race/national origin (U.S. Department of Education, 2009, p. 8).

Also in fiscal year 2008, OCR initiated 42 compliance reviews, the foci of which are listed below. The two categories in which the largest number of compliance reviews were conducted were athletics (with 16 reviews) and AP and Other High-Level Learning Opportunities (with 5 reviews) (see Figure 4.1.)

Though limited in number, OCR compliance reviews are exhaustive in scope, often producing several hundred pages of findings. Few schools or districts have the capacity to voluntarily conduct equity-focused investigations of their programs at the level of an official OCR review. Thus, the concept of equity audits that we have developed and refined through our

Figure 4.1   OCR Compliance Reviews, by Issue FY 2008

Accessibility (Section 504, ADA Title II)
Admission (Title VI)
AP and Other High-Level Learning Opportunities (Title VI)
AP and Other High-Level Learning Opportunities (Section 504, ADA Title II)
AP and Other High-Level Learning Opportunities (Multiple Jurisdiction)
Assignment of Student (Section 504, ADA Title II)
Athletics (Title IX)
Discipline (Title VI)
Free Appropriate Public Education (FAPE) (Section 504, ADA Title II)
Limited–English Proficient Students and Special Education / Services for Students with Limited–English Proficiency (Title VI, Section 504, ADA Title II)
Minorities and Special Education (Title VI, Section 504, ADA Title II)
Procedural Requirements (Title IX)
Procedural Requirements (Section 504, ADA Title II)
Procedural Requirements (Multiple Jurisdictions)

Source: U.S. Department of Education, 2009, p. 13

series of books is grounded in equity concerns related to the work of the OCR, but our version is much more limited in scope and produces a more manageable volume of data.

Curriculum Auditing

A second area in U.S. education in which equity audits are found historically is curriculum auditing. Curriculum audits appeared on the U.S. education scene in the late 1970s as an education-focused offspring of the Total Quality Management movement in business and industry. Fenwick English is generally acknowledged to be the father of curriculum audits (originally termed *curriculum management audits*) in the U.S. (Frase, English, & Poston, 1995). The curriculum audit as framed by English and his colleagues focuses on five standard areas. Standard 3 is "A School System Demonstrates Internal Connectivity and Rational Equity in its Program Development and Implementation." Thus, a form of equity audits is included in every curriculum audit, though equity is not the single, or even main, focus of the traditional curriculum audit.

In 1992, William Poston and his colleague Jacqueline Mitchell used Standard 3 as the springboard for development of their own version of the school equity audit. Poston (1992) outlined 15 areas to be analyzed in the school equity audit (Figure 4.2). One report using this method for conducting school equity audits was published (Mitchell & Poston, 1992); this was a case study of three school districts. We were not able to locate additional published work applying this method for equity audits.

Figure 4.2   Poston's Areas of Analysis for School Equity Audits

1. Administrative and supervisory practices
2. Course offerings and access
3. Financial and funding sources
4. Individual difference considerations
5. Materials and facilities
6. Special program and services delivery
7. Student management practices
8. Class-size practices
9. Demographic distribution
10. Grouping practices and instruction
11. Instructional time utilization
12. Promotion and retention practices
13. Staff development and training
14. Support services provision
15. Teacher assignment and work load

Source: Poston, 1992, p. 236

Another version of school equity audits was developed by researchers studying math and science reform; this National Science Foundation funded work produced what Jane Kahle (1998) described as an *equity metric*. She and her colleagues used this equity metric to analyze racial and gender equity in mathematics and science in several schools (Hewson, Kahle, Scantlebury, & Davies, 2001). The equity metric developed by these researchers has 22 indicators grouped into four categories: access, retention, achievement, and overall (p. 1139).

Accountability

A third area in U.S. education, in addition to civil rights enforcement and curriculum auditing, in which our conceptualization of equity audits has roots is state accountability. Over the course of the past two decades, several states have developed, implemented, and (in some cases) abandoned processes and instruments to evaluate levels of equity and inequity in schools and districts within individual states. For example, Kentucky had a statewide equity assessment that was in use until several years ago. This instrument grew out of earlier work with curriculum auditing within Kentucky (Steffy, 1993).

Washington and Iowa also previously had state-level processes for equity auditing, with Washington providing a web-based tool for schools and districts to use and Iowa conducting onsite equity reviews in selected school districts annually. Both of these state-level processes have now been discontinued.

One state-level accountability instrument focused specifically on equity that is still in use is Texas's Performance-Based Monitoring System. According to the Texas Education Agency's website,

> The Performance-Based Monitoring Analysis System (PBMAS) . . . is an automated data system that reports annually on the performance of school districts and charter schools in selected program areas (bilingual education/English as a second language, career and technical education, special education, and certain Title programs under the No Child Left Behind Act. (Texas Education Agency, 2010)

The PBMAS produces publically available reports for districts, regions, and the state that show disaggregated achievement, placement, and completion data for students served through the programs referenced above.

REFINING EQUITY AUDITS INTO A USABLE TOOL

As illustrated in the sections above, the general concept of equity audits has a rich and significant history in the U.S. and in international settings, both inside and outside of the education field. These historical efforts to conduct equity audits formed the base for our work that began 10 years ago through a grant from the Ford Foundation to develop a more stream-lined version of the concept for use by school leadership practitioners. We felt a more refined version of equity audits was needed, because, in our experience as school leadership researchers who were former practitioners ourselves, existing versions of the audits (whether through civil rights enforcement, curriculum auditing, or state accountability) were too large in scope to be useful in a practical way for guiding day-to-day equity-focused leadership work in schools. That is, earlier versions of equity audits produced huge amounts of data that could prove overwhelming for school leaders trying to use the information to plan and implement improvement efforts. Although extremely detailed and voluminous reports on school and school district practices, procedures, and outcomes can be useful in specific circumstances, such as documenting potential civil rights viola-tions, they are less useful in the daily leadership of schools.

Thus, our concept of equity audits was developed to be a more focused version of auditing concentrated on a limited set of indicators. In our view, school leaders needed to have data for their schools and school districts displayed in a clear and understandable way that showed levels of equity and inequity in key areas. Therefore, after careful consideration of the types of data commonly available to school leaders and the areas in which equity/inequity would most clearly show problems in an entire system, we developed a model based on 12 indicators grouped into three areas: *programmatic equity, teacher quality equity,* and *achievement equity.* These areas can be understood as a simple formula, as shown in Figure 4.3.

We clearly understand that this formula is an extremely simple (what some of our critics have called simplistic) representation of what is needed to achieve equity in schools. We also understand well, based on our ongoing work in schools struggling to realize their equity goals, that such work is intensely complex, extremely difficult, and frustratingly dynamic (that is, constantly changing). However, school leaders and other people working to advance equity in schools have to begin with the current situation in their environments, and it is simply impossible to

Figure 4.3   A Simple Formula for Equity Audits

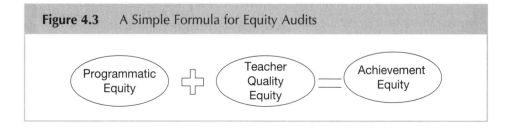

tackle everything all at once. Thus, our simplified model was designed to "chunk" an enormously complex and complicated situation into pieces of manageable size.

The 12 indicators that we selected for campus and district leaders to gather data on, work with stakeholder groups to analyze the data of, and develop plans for improvement for (grouped by category) are as follows:

Teacher Quality Equity

- Teacher education
- Teacher experience
- Teacher mobility
- Teacher certification

Programmatic Equity

- Special education
- Gifted and talented
- Bilingual education
- Discipline

Achievement Equity

- State achievement tests
- Dropout rates
- Graduation tracks
- SAT/ACT/AP/IB performance

This model for equity audits intended for use by school and school district leaders was the focus of our 2009 book for Corwin *Using Equity Audits to Create Equitable and Excellent Schools;* it is discussed and explained in greater detail there. We have included a brief description of it here, because it is part of the history of the development of the concept of equity audits that has lead us to the current discussion in this book of equity audits for classroom teachers.

CHAPTER CONCLUSION

A historical overview of equity auditing was presented in this chapter, including equity auditing at the international level and in U.S. education. Additionally, we discussed our version of equity auditing that was developed 10 years ago as a tool to be used by school leaders. This overview of equity audits was included to frame the context for our discussion in the next section—Equity Auditing for Classrooms. In this section, we discuss equity audits specifically as a tool to be used by teachers at the classroom level.

DISCUSSION QUESTIONS AND ACTIVITIES

1. For a deeper exploration of the concept of equity audits in U.S. civil rights enforcement, visit the U.S. Department of Education Office for Civil Rights website at http://www2.ed.gov/about/offices/list/ocr/index.html

2. Compare and contrast the equity audit concept for schools described in this chapter with other school improvement/planning processes that may be in use at your school.

3. For another approach to using data to identify inequities in schools and plan for improvement, see Ruth Johnson and Robin Avelar La Salle's (2010) Corwin book *Data Strategies to Uncover and Eliminate Hidden Inequities: The Wallpaper Effect*.

Section II

Equity Auditing in the Classroom

5 Auditing for Teaching and Learning

Instruction begins when you, the teacher, learn from the learner; put yourself in his place so that you may understand . . . what he learns and the way he understands it.

—Søren Kierkegaard

Like people, teaching and learning are complex. Moreover, there is an array of learning theories positing the best ways for students to learn and, as a result, the best ways for teachers to teach. These include, for example, problem-based learning (Barrows, 1986; Barrows & Tamblyn, 1980; Savery & Duffy, 1995), experiential learning (Kolb, 1984; Kolb & Fry, 1975.), self-directed learning (Brookfield, 1985, 1993, 2009; Caffarella, 1993; Knowles, 1975), critical thinking (Brookfield, 1993; Ennis, 1987), collaborative learning, (Johnson, Johnson, & Stanne, 1986), multiple intelligences (Gardner, 1983, 1999), learning styles (Kolb, 1981; Oxford, 1994), and the thinking curriculum (Resnick, 2010). Each of these theories addresses the complexities inherent in teaching and learning. Each has merit and is supported by research. In this chapter, we are *not* attempting to propose a new theory of learning. Rather, we are offering strategies for auditing whether teaching and learning are occurring, specifically auditing to ensure that each and every student is being taught and is learning, regardless of the learning theory one adheres to.

We believe that for students to learn, they have to be engaged. Explicitly, they need to be cognitively engaged, that is, engaged in thinking. We're not talking about just any kind of thinking, because we are almost always engaged in thinking. What we're referring to is thinking about the learning objective, being actively engaged in thinking about what the teacher is attempting to teach. We call this Active Cognitive

Engagement (ACE) (McKenzie & Lozano, 2008). This is different from merely being engaged. A student can be engaged without thinking about the learning objective. For example, collaborative or cooperative learning groups are viewed as a sound instructional strategy, and they can be. In these groups students are given a learning task to complete. The goal of the task is for students to learn a particular objective. However, what we often see in these learning groups is that one or two students are engaged in thinking about the learning objective, while the other students may be cognitively disengaged in regard to the learning objective. There typically is an effort to engage all students by assigning each student a role, such as leader, recorder, reporter, and so forth. Assigning roles is a good way to include all students in the process, working or collaborating together to accomplish a task or learning goal. However, working together may advance or may not advance the learning of a particular concept, skill, or strategy.

To illustrate, the student assigned to record the group's work may not have to think at all about the learning objective during collaborative group time. This student may only write down what the "thinking" students are directing the recorder to write. Thus, this student may spend the entire group time just hanging around waiting to record the other students' thinking. We realize this is a negative case example, and many teachers have effective collaborative or cooperative groups, but many do not. In these classrooms there is an appearance of engagement, and indeed all the students may be engaged at some point during the group activity, but the quality of ACE is low, because only a few students are doing the thinking work, that is, thinking about the learning objective. This is a loss of instructional and learning time for those students who are passive participants in the cooperative groups. Moreover, if these are the students who already have gaps in their learning or who are struggling with the new concept or objective being taught, which is often the case, the consequences of this loss of learning time can have negative effects, and over time, the effects of this cognitive disengagement can have devastating effects. Students who are not actively cognitively engaged may become bored and restless and, as a result, act out or acquiesce, giving up. If this continues day after day, month after month, year after year, one can easily see what can happen—students may become discipline problems, or they may mentally or physically just drop out.

The aforementioned example is one in which students are working, for the most part, on their own, although we realize in the best-case example, the teacher would be monitoring each group's activity. There are examples, however, of students not being actively cognitively engaged when the teacher is working directly with them in an effort to teach the students a new skill or concept. Let's take for example the first grade teacher who is teaching students to combine sets or add single digit numbers. We have observed in some classrooms where the teacher will put a numerical equation on the board, like 2 + 3 = ____. If the students are beyond the concrete operational stage, they will be asked to compute the answer. The teacher then asks who knows the answer. If the students are working with paper and pencil, some will immediately figure out the answer and raise their hands, eager to share. Some will have written the problem and not yet answered it, and some will not have the problem written down yet. The teacher will then call on one of the students who is volunteering an answer. If the student is correct, the teacher will say something like, "Nice job, did everyone get that?" Typically, some students will call out yes or shake their heads, and the teacher will move on to the next problem.

However, some of the students still may not even have the problem written down, some will not have answered the problem, and some will have answered the problem incorrectly. If this goes unnoticed, a gap opens or broadens. The teacher may think all the students got the correct answer, that all the students understand how to add. Moreover, the teacher may not discover that some of the students do not know how to add until there is a formal assessment. At this point, it may be too late to teach these students how to compute 2 + 3, because the teacher will have moved on to the next skill. One can see, then, that within the same classroom there can be students who are having two (or more) completely different learning experiences. This is a signal of inequity.

So, how can one ensure that students are actively cognitively engaged and that there is equity in the classroom, with equity defined as all students being actively cognitively engaged? We offer two strategies. One is helping teachers become aware of the level of ACE in their classrooms, and the other is helping teachers identify their Zone of Self-Efficacy (McKenzie & Lozano, 2008). The former, ACE, addresses teaching strategies, whereas the latter, Zone of Self-Efficacy, addresses teaching strategies along with the teacher's equity consciousness. (See chapters 2 and 3 for extensive discussions of high-quality teaching skills and equity consciousness.) What follows is the explanation of the ways we teach these strategies to teachers.

ACTIVE COGNITIVE ENGAGEMENT

To audit how much ACE there is in a classroom, teachers need to know which students are and are not engaged in thinking about the instructional objective being taught. This takes data. We have all taught something to students and watched as they nodded their heads in agreement, or perceived that students are engrossed in our lecture, demonstration, and so forth, only to discover later that the students did not understand what we were attempting to teach. Politeness and compliance do not mean students are actively cognitively engaged in the learning objective. To ensure that students are thinking and wrestling with the objective being taught, we need to see evidence of their thinking.

Let us explain by returning to our previous example of the first grade teacher who is attempting to teach students to add 2 + 3. Take a moment to consider what evidence or data would convince you that students, and we mean all students, are working the problem. Caution: We are not talking about evidence down the road, like results from a test. We are talking about how you know in this teaching moment that all your students have considered the problem and come up with an answer. Below are some of the strategies we have come up with for ensuring students are actively cognitively engaged. We use basically the same strategy for both elementary and secondary students. We are attempting here to show an easy way to change an unengaging lesson into an engaging one without a great deal of preparation.

Strategy One: Elementary Level

Each student is given a dry erase board. The problem $2 + 3 = $ ___ is posed. The students are to solve the problem and write their responses on the dry erase board. This requires all the students to consider the problem and answer it. Once they have the answer, they are to turn the board over. The teacher waits until all students have written their responses on their individual boards. Then the students are asked to hold up their boards and show their answers. Note: The boards should be held up at the same time toward the teacher. Doing this allows the teacher to assess immediately which students got the correct answer. If the students are at the concrete level—and all or some will be—instead of using a dry erase board, they can work the problem using cubes (manipulatives), cover their answers with their hands, and then show their answers when directed.

Once the teacher has posed several problems, the teacher can determine which students are having difficulty. Then, at that time or later in the day, the teacher can pull the struggling students into a small group to reteach them the concept. In other words, the teacher can address the gap right then and eliminate it. Of course, one reteach may not ensure the success of all the students, but repeated reteaching should. A question we always get is, "But, what will my other students be doing at this time?" Our response is that they can be working at centers or doing independent practice that challenges them with more complex problems. We aren't talking about working in a reteach group for long periods of time. Fifteen minutes in a small group should be sufficient.

Strategy Two: Secondary Level

Using a dry erase board may seem infantile to those who teach at the secondary level. However, we have used it in high schools with good results. For example, one teacher we worked with who teaches a sheltered instruction integrated physics and chemistry class used dry erase boards to play Jeopardy with her students. We had suggested this activity to her after observing her class and seeing over 50% of the students completely disengaged. She gave the Jeopardy activity a try, using it as a review for an upcoming test. It was highly successful in engaging all students.

Here's what she did. She divided the students into two teams. Each student had a dry erase board. Using PowerPoint, she displayed a Jeopardy-like screen that included categories of knowledge—like Properties of Solids—and point values under each category, just like the television show. First, a student from Team A picked the question, and the students on his team had a short time to write the answer. When the time was up, all students showed their answers. Points were awarded to the team for each correct answer. Points were taken away for any student who did not respond. (A student was assigned to keep a tally of the points.) Then, it was Team B's turn, and the process continued. One might argue that Team B was not cognitively engaged while Team A was answering their questions, and that may be true. However, the game moved quickly, and the level of ACE was very high. Therefore, there was far more ACE in this learning activity than there typically is when students watch a PowerPoint presentation and are asked to fill in a note-taking sheet, which is strategy we often see in secondary classes.

WHAT OUR CRITICS MIGHT SAY

Our critics might say that these examples represent rather low-level intellectual activities. We don't disagree, but we believe that the first step in getting students—particularly those students who have been disengaged for some time, even years—to think critically, to analyze, to synthesize, and to evaluate (Bloom, 1956) is to first get them thinking about what they are supposed to learn. Once they have developed a habit of mind that includes mentally answering the questions teachers are posing, they are on their way to engaging or reengaging with school. Unfortunately, we go into many classrooms and see students who are just sitting and are not engaged in any learning. We also see classroom instruction that doesn't require students to think or hold them accountable for thinking. Thus, we have to start here, getting students to think about what their teachers are asking them to consider or to do, getting teachers to construct rigorous lessons that are worth paying attention to, and getting teachers to teach all the students in their class (which we will address in the next section on the Zone of Self-Efficacy).

Therefore, to demonstrate that ACE can be used in a higher-order thinking lesson that requires students to intellectually engage at each level of Bloom's taxonomy (1956), from knowledge to evaluation, we offer an activity we do in one of our doctoral courses. Both of us teach a doctoral level class titled Models of Epistemology and Inquiry. It is the foundational research class in the doctoral curriculum. The students frequently comment that it is one of the most challenging courses in their program. In the class students learn about research paradigms like positivism, interpretivism, critical theory, poststructuralism, and so forth. Many of the terms they have to know and use are new to them. These include *epistemology*, *ontology*, *axiology*, and so on. It would be easy to disengage. However, in an attempt to practice what we preach, we work to cognitively engage our doctoral students just as we want K–12 teachers to engage their students.

One of the activities we use to engage students in discussing a challenging text they were required to read, Thomas Kuhn's *The Structure of Scientific Revolutions* (1970), is to pose a summary question for each chapter, a question that requires students to have a deep understanding of the chapter content. Note: The students are to read the entire text prior to this class meeting, which comes at the end of the semester. Initially, we divide the students into groups of no more than four or five. Next, each group is assigned one or two chapters for which they are to answer a question or questions. The questions are broad and usually address the main idea of the chapter. For example, in Kuhn's text the third chapter is titled "The Nature of Normal Science." The question we use for this chapter is, "What does Kuhn consider the nature of normal science?" The students are given 10 minutes to review, on their own[1], the chapters they were assigned and to answer the questions posed for each of their assigned chapters. At this point in the activity, the students are answering questions at the knowledge and/or understanding level of Bloom's taxonomy.

After the students have individually answered their questions, in their group they participate in a roulette activity. All students pass their answers to the first assigned chapter question to the student on their right. That student reads and responds to the original student's answer. Now the students have moved into the application and analysis phase, again according to Bloom's taxonomy. The response can be a question asking for clarification, an addition to or deletion from the original answer, a comment of disagreement, and so forth. Students then pass the question and responses on to the next person, who follows this same protocol. This continues until all students in the group have read and responded to all the other students' answers. When all students get back their original answers to the question, they read them and then as a group engage in an open conversation about the responses, leading toward the end task of deciding on one agreed-upon answer to the question, the synthesis phase. This answer is put on a wall chart, and once all groups have posted their answers, each group presents their responses to the summary questions. When one group shares, the other students in the class are assigned to comment on, challenge, and critically assess the quality of the response, thus extending everyone's learning and moving, finally, into the evaluation phase.

Here then is an example of using an ACE strategy that utilizes each of the levels of Bloom's taxonomy (1956) to engage doctoral students in substantive discussion around a challenging text. Therefore, as you can see, these ACE strategies can be used at any academic level and at any level of Bloom's taxonomy of intellectual behaviors, from knowledge to evaluation. We will return to this concept of ACE at the end of this chapter with a professional development activity to help you and your colleagues develop your own ACE strategies. Next we will discuss another technique for ensuring equity and excellence in the classroom—the Zone of Self-Efficacy.

ZONE OF SELF-EFFICACY

Whereas ACE involves using teaching strategies to engage all students, the Zone of Self-Efficacy addresses teacher attitudes that can potentially affect the engagement of students and thus the equity and excellence in the classroom. To explain, we'll take you through the professional development activity we do with teachers to help them understand Zone of Self-Efficacy.

First, though, we need to define terms. *Efficacy* is the belief in the power to achieve a desired outcome or goal. *Self-efficacy* as defined by Bandura (1994, p. 71) is "people's beliefs about *their* capabilities to produce effects" [emphasis added]. An efficacy statement is, "All students can learn." A self-efficacy statement is, "*I* can get *all* the students in my class to learn." The former is broad, and the later is specific, requiring agency on the part of the teacher.

The following is the activity we do with teachers. For this activity, teachers need their class list, pen or pencil, and a blank sheet of paper. Here's the script:

1. Looking at your class list, write down the names of the students you find easy to teach.

2. Now, using your class list, write down the names of the students you find most difficult to teach.

3. Next, look at your lists and determine what are the common characteristics of the "easy to teach" students? [We typically have teachers
just share this aloud.]

4. What are the common characteristics of the "more difficult to
teach" students? [We typically have teachers just share this aloud.]
[Note: The characteristics may be different for each teacher. This
process is about teachers determining their individual self-efficacy,
their beliefs about who they can and may not be able to teach. This
may be different for each teacher. Some teachers find high-energy
boys difficult to teach; some love them.]

5. Now draw a circle the size of an orange on your paper. Put the
names of the students you find easy to teach inside the circle.

6. Put the names of the students you find difficult to teach outside the
circle.

7. Before we proceed, we need to define two terms, *efficacy* and
self-efficacy. [Note: At this point we define the terms just as we did
at the beginning of this section.]

8. What you have determined is your Zone of Self-Efficacy [see Figure
5.1]. Those students inside your circle are the ones you may feel
confident you can teach. Those outside the circle are the students
that are difficult for you to teach, and you may feel that you cannot
teach these students unless something changes that makes these
students easier to teach. These changes may include getting the
students' parents to provide more help with homework, having
the principal or assistant principal involve themselves more in the
discipline of these students, getting the students to come to school
regularly, having the students assessed for learning difficulties or
attention problems, and so forth.

9. Finally, look critically at who is in and out of your zone. What
characteristics are common to the students who are in your zone
and what characteristics are common to the students who are out
of your zone? We know that there may be common behavior characteristics that make some students easier or harder to teach; but
look to see if there are any sociocultural factors. Are the students
who are in or out of your zone of the same race, culture, or ethnic
group? Are they of the same gender? Are they students whose
home language is something other than English? Are they students
who receive services through special education? [Note: These are
just a sampling of questions that can be posed; there may be others
depending on the context of the school.]

10. Now, reflect on your class. Is your class physically arranged so that it "looks like" your zone? In other words, if someone came into your class, could they "see" who you are teaching and who you are not teaching? Which students sit near the front of the class? Which ones sit at the back? Who do you call on? Which students are allowed to call out without raising their hands, and which are punished if they do? Who is in time-out or sitting outside the classroom? Who is allowed to sleep? At the extreme levels, who is no longer showing up at all; in other words, who has dropped out?

The purpose of having teachers determine their Zone of Self-Efficacy is to help them become sensitive to how they, typically unconsciously, include and exclude certain students or certain groups of students in their daily instruction. Indeed, this is an equity issue. All students deserve to have high-quality instruction. If teachers are concerned with equity, they need to determine ways in which they can expand their Zones of Self-Efficacy to include all students. This is a different mindset from that of waiting on external factors, like parents helping with homework, to change before a student is welcomed into the zone. In this new mindset teachers embrace the third belief that characterizes equity consciousness—that the adults in school are primarily responsible for student learning. Put bluntly, we cannot wait on students, student families, or the community to change before we teach the students we find difficult to teach. It is up to us to figure out how to include all our students in our zones. We realize this is a simple statement but a very difficult thing to do. One way we have helped

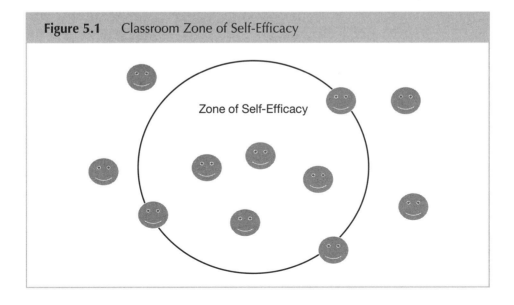

Figure 5.1   Classroom Zone of Self-Efficacy

teachers accomplish this feat is by providing them with the opportunity to engage in reflective practice and collegial conversation around the two concepts we discussed in this chapter: Active Cognitive Engagement and Zone of Self-Efficacy. We do this through a professional development activity and auditing tool we call Teaching and Learning Tours.

AN AUDITING TOOL: TEACHING AND LEARNING TOURS

We have used Teaching and Learning Tours as an auditing tool with great success in elementary and secondary schools in large urban districts, suburban districts, and rural districts. This is an easy and inexpensive way to provide in-situ (during the school day) professional development that can significantly impact the quality of teaching and learning in individual classrooms, schools, and school districts. Moreover, it focuses on the two concepts we addressed in this chapter—Active Cognitive Engagement and the Zone of Self-Efficacy. Here's how we have used this.

First, we introduce the teachers to ACE and the Zone of Self-Efficacy as explained above. We have done this in afterschool meetings or during teachers' planning or teaming periods during the day. Once the teachers have an understanding of these concepts, we introduce Teaching and Learning Tours. We explain that we will be taking small groups of teachers into each other's classrooms to look at teaching and learning. We make it very clear that *this is not an evaluation of the teacher and the teacher's teaching.* It is an opportunity for teachers to get together to engage in reflective practice. To do this, we need a laboratory or classroom; this is the reason we will be going into each other's classroom. We make it very explicit that we can't judge what's going on in a teacher's classroom, because we will only be in the room for 10 or 15 minutes. We don't know what went on in the room prior to our entry, and we don't know what will go on once we have left. The goal is for teachers to be able to stand at the back of a room and see the big picture. When teaching we are always in the trees, but when we go into someone else's classroom, we can actually see the forest. The best way to illustrate this is by explaining the form we use when conducting these Teaching and Learning Tours (see Figure 5.2 on page 56 at the end of this chapter).

As we stated previously, when we do these tours with teachers, we explain that this is not about evaluation. Next, we tell teacher-observers that we are going into classrooms and that they are to be as unobtrusive as possible—they are not to disturb instruction. They are to look at the classroom as if it were their own. In other words, they are to complete the observation form from the point of view of—"If this were my classroom, I. . . ." We really emphasize this point, because the purpose of the tour is for teachers to reflect on their own practice. So, starting with the first set of questions, "If this were your classroom, what would you be proud of?" and "What is positive in this classroom?" teachers are expected to look around the room and note what is going well, the things that impress them. This starts the observation and later discussion off on a positive tone and brings to the forefront the good things that are occurring.

Next, the teachers are asked, "What is the objective being taught?" This is important, because if one cannot discern the objective being taught, one can't answer the subsequent questions about ACE and the zone. Once this is completed, the teachers go on to the next question, "Based on this objective, what is the percentage of students that are actively cognitively engaged?" This question really gets at the first issue: How many kids are demonstrating that they are cognitively engaged in the learning objective? Teachers may get uncomfortable completing this question in that they are asked to actually put a number, a percentage to their response. To be clear, we are asking teachers, here, to count the number of students in the classroom and then quantify how many students are demonstrating learning. This is tricky. We often want to assume that if students are looking at the teacher and behaving, then they are attending and moreover thinking about and wrestling with the learning objective, but as we explained earlier that is not always the case.

So, what we are looking for with this question is, for example, when the teacher poses a question, how many students are required to answer it? Is the teacher calling on one student at a time? If so, do we have evidence that the other students have mentally, cognitively, answered that question? If the teacher being observed is using the one-on-one questioning strategy, we would say there is low evidence of ACE. However, if the teacher is asking a question and students are having to respond using dry erase boards, or with manipulatives, or through written responses, or in an array of other ways, then there is evidence that each student is having to consider the answer to the question. These students are developing a habit of mind that if the teacher asks them a question, they are to consider it. Too often, a teacher asks a question, one or two students respond, and the teacher moves on, thinking the entire class understands. And the gap opens. Now, the example we gave is for an observation of a direct instruction lesson, but evidence of cognitive engagement can also be ascertained when students are doing inquiry work, guided practice, or independent practice.

On to the next questions, "Are there any students out of the zone? If so, why do you think this is the case?" For these questions, teachers are to look around the room and note if any students are just not with the teacher, and the teacher is making no effort to get the student back into the zone. The observers should take note of students sitting in time-out, students who are sleeping, students who are trying to participate but are being overlooked, or students who are just zoning out. This is a critical observation. Teachers have told us that it was very clear who was or was not "with" the teacher. Moreover, they have said that this really opened their eyes to the possibility that they have unconsciously been excluding or just not noticing students that were not in these teachers' own zones. This is a big *ah ha!* for many.

The final question, "If this were your classroom, what would you do to ratchet up the ACE or ensure that all students were in the zone?" is answered once we leave the classroom. Thus, once the teachers have completed the observation form, answering all but the final question, we move out of the classroom into the hallway or another convenient location to debrief. In that debriefing, we go through each question, and the observers share their answers. This leads to fruitful conversation, particularly when discussing the level of ACE, where teachers may disagree on the levels or where some teachers may want to assert that students don't really have to respond to their questions for them to know that the students are engaged—they can tell by the looks on the students' faces whether the students "got it" or not. So, there is lots of friendly debate and usually some good insights that come from this question.

When the teachers get to the last question, they offer up strategies for improving the level of engagement or getting students in the zone. If the classroom had high levels of engagement, then the teachers discuss the ways the observed teacher accomplished this. In our experience with these tours, teachers have generated amazing strategies to increase ACE and prevent students from being out of the zone. We often compile these lists and share them at a faculty meeting. Additionally, it's important to explain that we don't just go into one classroom, we continue these tours so that we get into two or three classrooms. This can be done within a 45- or 60-minute conference or teaming period so that there is no need to hire substitute teachers, and teachers are not pulled out of their classrooms during instructional time.

The ultimate goal is for teachers to be mindful of their teaching while they are teaching, to audit their instruction for equity and excellence by asking themselves, "Who is engaged or not engaged? Is anyone out of the zone?" Secondarily, the goal is to give teachers a set of strategies they can use in their classrooms both to improve the ACE and to prevent students from being out of the zone. When we first began these tours, once we finished discussing the questions we asked teachers to go back to their rooms and try out the strategies they had generated. Some did, but many did not. This is just human nature. We as teachers are busy and are juggling enormous demands moment by moment, so we may have the intention to try something new or make our practice better, but the daily demands of the job seem to derail our efforts. We fall back on routine and our usual patterns.

Therefore, we realized we had to add another step to this professional development activity, an accountability measure. We know many of you are sick of hearing about accountability, but we believe being held accountable really makes a difference. It's the theory behind Weight Watchers, meditation groups, exercise boot camps, and so forth. So, we added the bottom portion to the observation tool, which asks teachers to decide which of the strategies that were generated they would like to try out in their classrooms and when they would like someone to come into their classrooms and give them feedback as to how well the strategy was working in regard to raising the level of ACE and getting all students in the zone. The person who observes the teacher's classroom and gives feedback can be another teacher, a department chair, a professional development specialist, or the principal. Regardless of who observes, it should be someone the teacher has a positive relationship with, and both parties need to understand this is *not* about evaluation but rather coaching. This is a professional development activity. Moreover, these tours are conducted throughout the year; they are not a one-time professional development activity. Initially, they need to be led by someone who is experienced in doing the tours and who can guide the discussion so that the observers can clearly see examples and non-examples of ACE and the zone. However, others on the campus can be trained to do this. We've used a trainer of trainers model and taught team leaders, department chairs, and teachers to lead the tours.

The benefits of these tours include more collegiality, transparency of instruction, improved teaching skills and equity consciousness, and the development of a professional learning community. Furthermore, the tours don't stop once there are high levels of ACE and all the students are in the zone. There are always new teachers that will need to develop these strategies, and we are always needing to continually improve our art. Thus, once a teacher or a campus feels confident with ACE and the zone, they can move on to other skills like instructional rigor.

CHAPTER CONCLUSION

This first chapter in the section on equity auditing focused specifically on teaching and learning, whereas the remaining chapters in this section address discipline, parental involvement, and programmatic issues.

Although equity issues related to discipline and programs, like special education and gifted and talented, address over- or underrepresentation of students within these areas, equity in teaching and learning is concerned with who gets taught and how well they are taught, period. Therefore, we began this chapter with a brief review of the literature on learning theories and then made the case that regardless of which theory or theories one embraces, students are not learning if they are not engaged in the teaching and learning process. Simply put, if students aren't "with us," they aren't learning. If they aren't learning, we aren't teaching.

To help determine which students are or are not with us, the concepts of Active Cognitive Engagement and the Zone of Self-Efficacy were introduced. Strategies to ensure ACE and that all students are in the teacher's Zone of Self-Efficacy were provided. Additionally, the auditing tool of Teaching and Learning Tours was discussed as a professional development activity to increase teachers' self-reflection in the area of assessing the equity in their classrooms. In the next chapter we address auditing for discipline.

DISCUSSION QUESTIONS AND ACTIVITIES

1. Reflect on the most recent professional development training session you attended. Did the presenter or trainer use strategies to monitor the level of ACE among all the participants in the training? If so, what strategies were used, and how might you use similar ones in your classroom? If not, what type of strategies might have been used? How might the use of such strategies have changed your level of engagement with the professional development being presented and the degree to which you benefitted from the session?

2. Have you ever had an experience as a student yourself in which you felt as if you were clearly outside the teacher's Zone of Self-Efficacy? If so, how did it feel to be on the outside of the zone? Did you realize this was happening at the time? Do you understand why you might have been outside the zone of students this teacher felt capable of teaching?

3. As a practice activity for the Teaching and Learning Tours described in this chapter, search YouTube for video clips of teachers teaching in K–12 classrooms. Use the handout provided in Figure 5.2, and try to answer those questions about the classroom in the YouTube clips that you find. Can you tell which students are cognitively engaged with the teacher? Is it obvious which students are inside or outside of the teacher's Zone of Self-Efficacy?

NOTE

1. In an effort to ensure that every student is cognitively engaged in the activity, we usually require students to first answer questions by themselves, then share in a small group, then with the whole class. This increases the likelihood that students will intellectually engage with the learning instead of sitting back and letting others do the thinking.

Figure 5.2   Teaching and Learning Tours

Focus: Active Cognitive Engagement; Zone of Self-Efficacy

Reminder: This is *not* about the person being observed. It *is* about using your colleague's classroom as a lab for you to engage in *reflective practice*—that is, thinking about your practice.

1. If this were your classroom, what would you be proud of? What is positive in this classroom?

2. What is the objective being taught?

3. Based on this objective, what is the percentage of children who are actively cognitively engaged?

4. Are there any students out of the zone? If so, why do you think this is the case?

5. If this were your classroom, what could you do to ratchet up the ACE? Or, ensure that all students are in the zone?

_____

When an observer comes to your classroom, he or she will give feedback on the strategies you want to try in your classroom. Which strategy or strategies do you want feedback on?

Teacher name: _____

6 Auditing for Discipline

Do not train children to learning by force and harshness, but direct them to it by what amuses their minds, so that you may be better able to discover with accuracy the peculiar bent of the genius of each.

—Plato

Ensuring that every student is taught and taught well is paramount to individual student success, schoolwide success, and, we would argue, the success of our nation and beyond. However, teaching all students well is not easy. As we demonstrated in the previous chapter, there are some students that teachers find easier to teach than others. It takes less effort to engage these students and keep them in the "zone." Conversely, there are some students that teachers find difficult to teach. It is harder to engage these students and thus keep them in the zone. Some of these students may even misbehave, creating discipline problems. However, although one teacher's difficult student may be another teacher's dream student, there are, according to research, some student groups nationwide who are disproportionately disciplined; that is, they are disciplined more often than other groups, even when they make up a smaller percentage of students within a classroom or school. These include boys (Mendez & Knoff, 2003), racial minorities (Brooks, Schiraldi, & Zidenberg, 1999; Costenbader & Markson, 1998; Skiba, Michael, Nardo, & Peterson, 2002; The Civil Rights Project, 2000), and students from low-income homes (Nichols, Ludwin, & Iadicola, 1999; Skiba et al., 2002; Theriot, Craun, & Dupper, 2010). Therefore, before we consider auditing for discipline disproportionality in an individual classroom, it's important to get a sense of the scope, the severity, and, ultimately, the consequences of the problem of discipline disproportionality. To do this, we'll turn to the research.

RESEARCH ON DISCIPLINE

As stated above, the three groups that are disproportionally disciplined are boys, racial minorities, and students from low-income homes. In regard to gender, boys are referred to the school office for disciplinary infractions more often than girls. Skiba and his colleagues (2002), in a study of over 11,000 students in 19 middle schools in a large urban midwestern school district, found that boys are more likely than girls to be referred to the office for an array of offenses, ranging from minor to severe. The only category in which girls were more likely to be referred than boys was truancy. In addition to gender, students from some racial groups, particularly blacks[1], are disproportionally disciplined. According to the U.S. Department of Education[2] for the year 2004–2005, in regard to suspension and expulsion (the two most severe disciplinary consequences), blacks were suspended and expelled at a ratio that is approximately two times their representation in schools (see Figure 6.1).

For example, if blacks made up 25% of a school population, they composed 50% of the suspensions and expulsions for that school. Thus, they were overrepresented or disproportionately suspended and expelled. Additionally, they were suspended and expelled 3.1 and 2.9 times more often than whites, respectively. This research also showed that, nationwide, Hispanics were suspended and expelled at rates that were approximately proportionate to their representation in schools. In other words, they were not overrepresented in these disciplinary consequences. However, in some states Hispanic students were overrepresented in disciplinary actions, including suspensions and expulsions. Whites, on the other hand, were underrepresented. So, if whites made up 25% of the school population, they composed less than 25% of the suspensions and expulsions.

Not only are some student groups more often and more severely disciplined than others, the raw numbers of students in general who are suspended or expelled are alarming. According to the National Center for Education Statistics (NCES, 2009), "In 2006, about 1 out of every 14 students (or 7 percent) was suspended from school at least once during the year" (p. 1). It's important to note that these statistics did not include

Figure 6.1 National Discipline Statistics

Ratio of Suspensions to Enrollment					Ratio of Expulsions to Enrollment				
Black	White	Hispanic	Black/ White	Hispanic/ White	Black	White	Hispanic	Black/ White	Hispanic/ White
2.2	0.7	1.0	3.1	1.3	2.0	0.7	1.1	2.9	1.5

Source: U.S. Department of Education, 2004.

in-school suspensions. Moreover, the total number of students suspended in 2006 was 3.3 million, and the total number of students expelled was 102,100 (NCES, 2009). Furthermore, if these numbers aren't staggering enough, one should also keep in mind that the suspension and expulsion rates are higher for male and black students. For example, in 2006, 15% of black students were suspended compared to 5% of white students, and 0.3% of black students were expelled from school compared to 0.1% of white students (NCES, 2009). Therefore, in our schools today, we have substantial numbers of students who for disciplinary reasons are not in our classrooms, with the highest percentage of these students being male and black. Moreover, "When the American Psychological Association (APA) reviewed popular zero-tolerance discipline policies in 2006, it found no evidence that suspension, expulsion, or zero-tolerance policies resulted in improvements in student behavior or enhanced school safety" (Southern Poverty Law Center, 2009).

It is not, though, just these severe levels of discipline in which black students are overrepresented. Black students, particularly black male students, are more often referred for disciplinary actions and referred for offenses that are subjectively determined. For example, Skiba et al. (2002) found that white students are more often referred to the office for "an objective event (e.g., smoking, vandalism) that leaves a permanent product"; whereas black students are more often referred for "infractions (e.g., loitering, excessive noise) that would seem to require a good deal more subjective judgment on the part of the referring agent" (p. 334). One has to wonder why this would be the case. One explanation, historically offered, is that neither race nor gender is the predictive factor; rather it is socioeconomic level. However, Skiba et al.'s (2002) research found that gender and race were more predictive of disciplinary referrals than socioeconomic level. Moreover, they found that "while white students and teachers perceived racial disparity in discipline as unintentional or unconscious, students of color saw it as conscious and deliberate, arguing that teachers often apply classroom rules and guidelines arbitrarily to exercise control, or to remove students whom they do not like" (Skiba et al., 2002, p. 335).

Certainly, none of us want to believe that we are unjust, but the research is hard to deny—students of color, and particularly boys, are more often disciplined and more harshly disciplined than their white counterparts. This has become clear to us in our experiences working in and with schools. We often see students isolated in the back of the room, or sitting outside classrooms in the hallway, or roaming around the campus, or waiting to see the assistant principal for disciplinary action, or sitting in in-school suspension. Moreover, most of the time, these students are black or Latino/a, even when the majority of the school is white. There is a disproportionate number of students of color, mainly black, who are disciplined. This means that these students are more often out of the learning environment. This is a problem.

Citing the work of teaching and learning scholars, Gregory, Skiba, and Noguera (2010) contend, "One of the most consistent findings of modern education research is the strong positive relationship between time engaged in academic learning and student achievement (Brophy, 1988; Fisher et al., 1981; Greenwood, Horton, & Utley, 2002)" (p. 60). If a student is not at school due to suspension or expulsion, or if a student is at school but is not in the classroom because the student is either in in-school suspension or waiting in the office to see a school administrator regarding a disciplinary issue, then the student is not engaged in academic learning. Research is clear; disciplinary actions that take students out of the classroom, like suspension, affect achievement (Davis & Jordan, 1994). Moreover, suspension has been shown to be a predictor of students dropping out of school or not graduating on time (Raffaele Mendez, Knoff, & Ferron, 2002). If we know that black students, and, in some states, Latino/a students, are more often suspended, and we look at the achievement levels of these students and their rates of dropping out or delayed graduation, it appears there is a correlation.

REASONS FOR DISCIPLINE DISPROPORTIONALITY

Gregory et al. (2010) call the disproportionality of discipline the "racial discipline gap." In an effort to explain the reasons given for this gap, they state,

> Certain demographic characteristics that are more common among some racial and ethnic groups have been used as a primary explanation for the racial discipline gap (see, e.g., National Association of Secondary School Principals, 2000). Low income students with histories of low achievement, who reside in high-crime/high-poverty neighborhoods, may be at greater risk for engaging in behavior resulting in office disciplinary referrals and school suspension. A review of the literature suggests that such characteristics likely account for some proportion of the gap in sanctions across groups. Yet there is *no* evidence to suggest demographic factors are in any way sufficient to "explain away" the gap. Teachers and school factors need to be considered as possible contributors to the over-selection and oversanction of Black, Latino, and American Indian students. (p. 61, emphasis added).

We addressed the *school factors* for the racial and gender discipline gap in our previous book, *Using Equity Audits to Create Equitable and Excellent Schools.* In this text our focus is on *teacher and classroom factors* regarding this gap. We know that boys, and blacks, and in some places, Latino/a and American Indian students are more often and more severely disciplined than other students. We know that these disciplinary measures take students out of the learning environment. Furthermore, we know that being out of the classroom negatively affects learning. Therefore, if we want to ensure high levels of success for all students—that is, if we want to close the achievement or learning gap—we must look critically at our classroom practices to see if we are disciplining students disproportionally; if so, we need to examine why this is occurring. It may be that a student is struggling with issues outside of school, or with peer relationships, or with not having the requisite skills to understand what is being taught, or with a learning style that is not being addressed, or with not being engaged in a rigorous curriculum. The first step, though, is to determine if there are disciplinary inequities in the classroom. What follows are strategies for auditing disciplinary actions in the classroom to determine if there is disproportionality.

AUDITING TOOLS FOR EXAMINING CLASSROOM DISCIPLINARY PRACTICES

As we have said repeatedly, and as research attests (see, for example, Argyris & Schön, 1974; Schön, 1983, 1987), teacher reflective practice is critical for examining attitudes and practices that ensure equity. In regard to discipline, we offer three auditing tools to assist in this reflection. The first is a reflective survey designed to bring awareness to areas of possible inequity (see Figure 6.2 on page 65 at the end of this chapter).

In using this survey, read the questions and answer them as honestly as possible. This is a private survey, for your eyes only. So, reflect and answer as accurately as you can. And if in this self-reflection you discover that your practices may not be the way you wish they were, do not get caught up in guilt or self-deprecation. Self-reflection is not about feeling bad about ourselves or our actions; it is about honestly looking at ourselves and our actions and realizing there may be a need of improvement. As the saying goes, "Once you know better, do better."

The second tool is a discipline chart that allows teachers to keep track of who is disciplined, for what reasons, and to what severity (see Figure 6.3 on page 67 at the end of this chapter). In using this chart, you should record each disciplinary incident—write the student's name, the offense, and the disciplinary action, and then complete the remaining demographic information. Review the chart daily or weekly looking for patterns. Is one child repeatedly being disciplined? Is one gender or one racial or ethnic group disciplined more often or more severely? How about students who receive services through special education or who are English language learners; are they disciplined more often or more severely? These data let you discern whether you are being equitable in regard to discipline. If so, great! If not, then again the often difficult but needed work of reflecting on one's thoughts and attitudes about certain students and student groups begins. We would caution though that you cannot really wait to understand the complexities involved in your thoughts before changing actions. We suggest changing actions while concurrently reflecting on attitudes.

So, if you realize that most of the students disciplined in the class are, for example, Latino/as, then you need to consider why. The simple answer may be, "Well they are the ones who most often misbehave." But, you need to go deeper. Why are they the ones that most often misbehave? Is it because they are having difficulty with the work? Are their instructional needs being met? Or, could it be that you have a bias related to Latino/as? Typically, this bias, which comes from an array of social, cultural, and familial influences, is unconscious. However, it is easy to see in a classroom. We have seen situations in which, for example, a white student will get up out of his seat to sharpen a pencil, and the teacher allows it. Then a Latino/a student gets up to do the same and is called down for breaking the rule against getting out of his seat during work time without permission. We realize in reading this you may think this is incredible, but it happens. Moreover, teachers are truly unaware that they are responding in this way. That's why auditing for equity in discipline is so important. It helps bring the unconscious to a conscious level so that issues of inequity can be addressed.

Last, we include a chart on family communication (see Figure 6.4 on page 68 at the end of this chapter). Like the Classroom Disciplinary Record, the Family Communication Chart is an auditing tool to help you in examining the frequency and quality of the communication you have with students' families regarding student behavior.

You can use this tool to periodically review, we recommend monthly at a minimum, your contact with students' families. The equity traps (McKenzie & Scheurich, 2004) to look for while using this chart include repeated negative communication to the same family and/or a pattern of negative feedback based on students' race, ethnicity, gender, participation in special education or Section 504 programs, and so forth. Becoming aware of these traps is the first step in freeing yourself from them. If you consistently and thoughtfully use these tools to audit for discipline, you should become more self-reflective about your equity practices regarding discipline.

CHAPTER CONCLUSION

We began this chapter with a quote from Plato. One has to wonder whether Plato and our other early academics had discipline issues with their students, since discipline always seems to be a topic with teachers and one that has been around since the inception of schools. In this chapter, though, we did not focus on discipline in general, but rather a specific equity issue related to discipline—the disproportional representation of some student groups among those who are disciplined. We began the chapter by explaining disproportionality and providing research on this topic. The need to audit our practices regarding whom we discipline, how frequently, and to what severity was discussed. Additionally, we offered three auditing tools to help you assess the equity in your discipline practices. These included the Reflective Survey About Classroom Practices, the Classroom Disciplinary Record, and the Family Communication Chart. The next chapter addresses auditing for parental involvement.

DISCUSSION QUESTIONS AND ACTIVITIES

1. If you were to take an informal survey of your teacher colleagues and ask about the relationship between learning and student discipline, would more of them agree with the statement, "A teacher must have good discipline in her/his room in order for students to learn" or the statement "A teacher's students must be learning in order for them to have good discipline"? What reasons would your colleagues likely give to support their answers?

2. If you were to walk around your school and observe students in disciplinary situations (waiting to see the assistant principal, in time-out, in in-school suspension), what conclusions could you draw about the school based solely on that observation? Do the students in disciplinary situations look like the students in the general population of the school? How many students would you see during any given class period outside of their regular classrooms, either in a disciplinary placement or waiting to receive disciplinary consequences for some infraction that had already occurred?

3. Are there teachers on your campus who seem to have little problem with discipline issues in their classrooms? Others that seem to have extraordinary difficulty with classroom discipline? What characteristics do the teachers in the group that has little problem with discipline seem to have in common? What characteristics do you see in common among the group of teachers who seem to struggle the most with discipline?

NOTES

1. Although we have used the term *African American* throughout this book, for this chapter we use the term *black*, because this is the term the researchers used in reporting their research on this population group.

2. As reported in the *Chicago Tribune e-Edition*. Retrieved from http://www.chicagotribune.com/services/newspaper/eedition/chi-070914discipline-html-story,0,809797.htmlpage

Figure 6.2	Reflective Survey About Classroom Practices

1. Do you have classroom procedures such as requiring students to raise their hands to ask a question or offer a comment? If so . . .
   - Do you allow some students to call out without consequence, but give a consequence to other students? Typically, which students are these?
     - What gender are they?
     - What racial and/or ethnic group do they belong to?
     - Are they students who receive services through special education or Section 504?
     - Are they students who come from low-income homes?
     - Are they English language learners (ELL students)?
   - Why do you think you require some students to follow the rules while not requiring others to attend to the rules?

2. When teaching, do you have procedures to ensure that you engage all students? For example, do you walk around the class, using proximity, to ensure that students are "with you?" If so . . .
   - Are there some students you make sure you engage and others that you allow to disengage? Typically, which students are these?
     - What gender are they?
     - What racial and/or ethnic group do they belong to?
     - Are they students who receive services through special education or Section 504?
     - Are they students who come from low-income homes?
     - Are they ELL students?
   - Why do you think you require some students to follow the rules, while requiring others to attend to the rules?

3. In reviewing your discipline referrals, which students are most often disciplined or referred to the office?
   - Have you considered the following?
     - What racial and/or ethnic group do they belong to?
     - Are they students who receive services through special education or Section 504?
     - Are they students who come from low-income homes?
     - Are they ELL students?
   - Why do you think you discipline or refer some students, or students from the same population group, more often than others?

4. In reviewing your discipline referrals or actions you take in the classroom regarding discipline, what are the student behaviors that resulted in your disciplinary actions?
   - Are these objective incidences, like damaging property or hurting another student?
   - Are these subjective incidences, like showing disrespect or disrupting the class?
   - Which students are disciplined more often for objective incidences, and which are disciplined more often for subjective incidences?
     - What gender are they?
     - What racial and/or ethnic group do they belong to?

Figure 6.2 (*Continued*)

 ○ Are they students who receive services through special education or Section 504?
 ○ Are they students who come from low-income homes?
 ○ Are they ELL students?

5. When you communicate to students' families, are there some students whose families you initiate communication with more frequently than others? If so . . .

 ● Is this communication positive or negative regarding the students' behavior?
 ● Which students or student groups receive the most negative communication?
 ● Why do you think this is?

Figure 6.3 Classroom Disciplinary Record

Student's Name	Date	Offense	Disciplinary Action	Student's Race/ Ethnicity	Student's Gender	Special Ed./504 Student?	ELL Student?	Low-Income Student?

Figure 6.4 Family Communication Chart

Student's Name	Date	Family Contact	Summary of Communication	Student's Race/Ethnicity	Student's Gender	Special Ed./504 Student?	ELL Student?	Low-Income Student?

7 Auditing for Parental Involvement

The community has a vital stake in the education of every child. Education is a common concern not merely because there are many children to be educated, but because there can be no significant outcome in the education of any child which is not of importance, not to him only, but also to others, immediately to many, more remotely to all.
—H. W. Holmes

A chapter on parental involvement might seem, at first glance, an odd fit among the other chapters included in this book on equity auditing at the classroom level. One might even ask how it is possible to audit levels of parental involvement. Nonetheless, there is almost universal agreement that parental involvement is important to student success in school (Lopez, 2001), and lack of or low levels of parental involvement is, almost without exception, among the top three reasons most teachers give for lack of equitable success across different groups of students in their classrooms (Bol & Berry, 2005). Thus, something as important as parental involvement cannot be left to chance. It, like the rest of the areas we have covered in this book, is something that can be assessed and analyzed through the process of equity audits and an area in which improvement strategies can be developed and implemented.

WHAT RESEARCH SAYS ABOUT PARENTAL INVOLVEMENT

A recent review of the literature on parental involvement in education conducted by SEDL explored the question, "Does parental involvement in children's schooling really matter?" The answer to this question, based on a systematic review of recent literature, was as follows:

> According to the research, the answer is yes. Sometimes, results come in more traditional measures—student achievement, attendance, or behavior. These measures tend to be based in schools and controlled by school staff. At other times, there are less traditional benefits, such as improved student or family self-efficacy about education, higher expectations for students or others involved in efforts, more effective ways to support family engagement, greater understanding of the viewpoints of others, or student planning for the future. These measures may be driven by the school, the home, the community, families, or students. The key is not that the source of additional student support comes from a specific entity, but that students benefit significantly when there is an individual encouraging and expecting the child to be academically successful. In fact, there is evidence that it is not "the parent" that makes the difference, but instead it is adults who take the time to talk to students, express an interest in their education, and hold them accountable for learning. This adult may be someone in the home, the school, or the community. Moreover, students of all ages benefit academically, emotionally, and physically when an adult is actively involved in the day-to-day events of their lives, including school activities. (Ferguson, 2008, p. 2)

Thus, according to SEDL researchers, significant involvement by an adult has a positive influence on both traditional academic outcomes and other desirable outcomes such as improved self-efficacy and higher educational aspirations.

It is important to emphasize here something the SEDL staff also pointed out—that the term *parental involvement* includes parents but also includes other adults who may be raising or caring for children, such as grandparents, other relatives, foster parents, and guardians. The point here is that significant involvement by a caring adult with a child's schooling has positive value. Therefore, when we use the phrase *parental involvement* in this chapter, we mean that term to include all adults who are involved in caring for children and supporting their education.

The SEDL review of the research organized its findings into six broad categories: sense of welcome, misconceptions among stakeholders, use of and issues related to resources, home context and student performance, program structures, and roles of those involved in school-family connections. Key findings in these areas that are relevant to equity auditing in classrooms are discussed briefly below (Ferguson, 2008, p. 24).

Sense of Welcome

SEDL defined sense of welcome as "creating a welcoming environment that fosters family-school relationships and transcends context, culture, and language" (Ferguson, 2008, p. 9). The basic finding from studies in this area was that parents and other significant adults are more likely to be engaged with the school when they feel welcome to do so. Welcoming parental involvement programs, however, are characterized by more than a general sense of friendliness. For a school to be truly welcoming of parental participation in children's education, it must also address specific parent and community needs and be respectful and appreciative of language and cultural differences (Washington Alliance for Better Schools, 2003).

As an example of successful strategies used to create a sense of welcome for parents at their children's schools, one of the authors (McKenzie) found it very important to attend to parents' language needs when she was principal at an elementary school serving a large population of Spanish-speaking immigrant families. The school was also located near a state school for the deaf. It was obvious to the school improvement planning team that parents would not feel welcome to attend PTO meetings, open houses, parent nights, family literacy activities, or any other gathering of parents at the school if they could not understand what was being said. Thus, it became standard practice at this school to have both a Spanish-English interpreter and an American Sign Language interpreter at schoolwide meetings for parents. This practice, somewhat remarkably, became a point of contention when a state dignitary visited the school to make a speech and objected to having her talk interpreted in Spanish! It might have annoyed the visiting VIP, but providing interpreters for parents was a tremendously successful strategy at this elementary school for improving the sense of welcome for literally all parents.

Misconceptions Among Stakeholders

Findings in this section center on the fact that school personnel's and families' misperceptions about each other's motivations, practices, and beliefs interfere with the development of functional school-home relationships. The widespread belief that some families just do not care about their children's education falls in this category. What teachers and others typically mean when they voice this belief is that parents of some of their students (typically families from low-income homes and families of color) do not participate in traditional school-centered parental involvement activities (joining the PTA/PTO, attending meet-the-teacher night) at the same level that families of other children do.

Despite the common belief that such lack of participation in traditionally structured activities translates into lack of caring, research shows that these same families most often care deeply about their children's education and success in school. Their caring and participation may not, however, be demonstrated in ways that teachers and others steeped in traditional schooling practices and paradigms recognize and understand. As Lopez (2001) pointed out,

> Unfortunately, research suggests that the vast majority of marginalized families fall in the "uninvolved" category (Chavkin, 1993; Moles, 1993). As a result, many have been judged to be unconcerned and perhaps uncaring, when in fact all these parents have "failed" to do was to become involved in normative ways (Clark, 1983; Lightfoot, 1978). Certainly, marginalized parents and family members are involved to a significant extent in the lives of their children, yet many of their activities are outside conventional understandings of involvement. In other words, involvement *can* consist of a number of different activities, but only a few of these activities are acknowledged in the educational arena. (pp. 417–418)

In Lopez's research with migrant families, he found that the parents who participated in his study taught their children the value of hard work and explicitly communicated the expectations that their children become educated so they could have a wider range of employment options than their parents did. Lopez defined both of these familial teachings as parental involvement in education that existed outside the boundaries of traditional understandings of what parental involvement means.

Use of and Issues Related to Resources

Findings from research on parental involvement around use of resources typically discuss two types of resources—those provided by schools and those provided by parents and families. The conclusion drawn by the SEDL researchers in this area is that, regardless of where the resources come from, "when resources are directed to support specifically targeted areas of need, there is greater support for student learning" (Ferguson, 2008, p. 13). In other words, a focused and coherent approach to targeting parental involvement resources, regardless of source, leads to better support for learning in classrooms.

An example of how a school responded effectively to the challenge of increasing parental involvement was provided recently in a class discussion involving several of our doctoral students. One of the students (who is an elementary principal) described holding a meeting of parent leaders at his school at the beginning of the year to discuss ways parents could support students' learning. He was expecting to discuss holding evening sessions for parents to focus on reading and math strategies, or providing parenting classes, or some sort of tried-and-true parental involvement activities. When he finished his remarks to the parents and turned to ask the parents what they wanted from the school, they replied, "Crosswalks and crossing guards." When the other students in our graduate class asked this principal how he responded to the parents' request, he said, "I worked with the city to get crosswalks painted and worked with the PTO to coordinate volunteer crossing guards."

In other words, this principal was wise enough to understand that when he asked parents what they needed from the school, and they told him, he needed to honor their requests by targeting resources toward solving their most pressing issues. This built trust between the school and the parents that could later serve as the foundation for moving on to some of the activities the principal was interested in having parents participate in that fell into more traditional definitions of parents supporting students' learning.

Home Context and Student Performance

The research literature in this area focuses on the connections between children's school performance and the kind of context for learning that is present in the home. In an increasingly diverse society, it is critical to recognize that narrow, stereotypical conceptions of what kind of home context is required to be considered a "supportive" home are unrealistic and not helpful to school personnel who are genuinely interested in creating functional school-home connections. The SEDL researchers summed this point up this way:

> Although this collection of studies continues to recognize a common list of activities that nurture learning at home—provide study time and space and help with homework—fostering home-based learning support is too complex of a process to be "fixed" by actions on a list. (Ferguson, 2008, pp. 14–15)

Other researchers, including Delgado-Gaitan (1992), have long advocated for the necessity of educators recognizing and respecting students' home contexts as important sources of support for students' education, even and especially when those contexts differ from those of the teachers.

Program Structures

Recent research on program structures to support parental involvement shows that programs or parental outreach activities that are sporadic, unfocused, or largely symbolic in nature are unlikely to be effective. Like virtually every topic we have addressed in this book, figuring out how to create program structures that will actually support parental involvement rather than just be a showpiece is messy and hard work. The SEDL report emphasizes this point:

> As programs create structures to prepare educators and families for meaningful family engagement, there are complex and often difficult issues that will need to be addressed:
>
> - Confronting both conscious and subconscious bias
>
> - Instilling processes that encourage and prepare families to model effective strategies and to foster family/child bonding and high performance expectations
>
> - Encouraging educators and families to address the needs of the whole child, not just the academic needs
>
> - Incorporating procedures to collect useful data to determine effectiveness and evaluate family satisfaction with the structures and procedures (Ferguson, 2008, pp. 18–19)

In other words, there is no one-size-fits-all formula for effective parental involvement programs. Successful programs are developed in partnership with local parents and communities and build on the strengths, interests, and needs of parents, students, and school staff (National Coalition for Parent Involvement in Education, 2004).

One example of a successful program structure that supported increased levels of parental involvement in successful school districts that we studied came from a highly experienced parental involvement coordinator that one district in our study had hired when it became clear that increased levels of parental participation were key to accomplishing the district's goals. This coordinator explained her strategy for getting past the typical barriers that prevented high levels of parental involvement with schools in this way:

> Your target population is going to be all those parents that think they're a nothing, all the parents that think they have nothing to offer, all those parents who think their children can't learn, all those parents that have given up. . . . They're going to be polite, and so they'll give you excuses. So you knock down the barriers.

In my model, we knock down the barriers. There's going to be transportation for them, childcare. At the parent's center they can go ahead and bring the children. . . . You knock down the barriers. (Skrla, Scheurich, & Johnson, 2000, p. 36)

This award-winning educator focused her approach to structuring support for parental involvement at the district level on removing well-known barriers to parental participation in her primarily low-income community. Similar strategies might be appropriate for teachers to consider at the classroom level.

Roles of Those Involved in School-Family Connections

The studies SEDL reviewed in this area point to the importance of role clarity in supporting effective parental involvement. That is, both the school personnel and family members need a clear understanding of what they are supposed to do and what they can expect of the other people involved in supporting the children's education. The authors explain the situation this way:

Often the most voiced concerns in defining family roles stems from the differing perspectives of educators and noneducators. Family members' perceptions of self-efficacy related to language and socioeconomic status are often significant factors in how families determine their roles in their children's education, just as they are in the teachers' preconceptions about the role of the family. (Ferguson, 2008, p. 20)

It is important to understand that much of what goes on under the umbrella of parental involvement (as well as judgments made by educators about parental noninvolvement) is guided by unexamined assumptions about who is supposed to be doing what or who is capable of or interested in doing what. For example, Weiss et al. (2003) recommended gathering information about families' work schedules and afterschool arrangements so that opportunities for formal and informal parental involvement could be scheduled at times and in settings that maximized the likelihood that parents could actually attend.

CLASSROOM PARENTAL INVOLVEMENT INVENTORY

Much of the research literature on parental involvement reviewed in the previous section focused on school-level programmatic activity to support school-family connections. Moreover, in our previous book, *Using Equity*

Audits to Create Equitable and Excellent Schools, we offer several strategies for increasing parental connections and involvement at the school level. These include positive phone calls to students' homes, home visits, and schoolwide neighborhood walks. However, in addition to whatever is occurring at the school or school district level to support parental involvement in children's education, the most important point of interface between the school and home is individual teachers' classrooms. The classroom level is also the focus of this book, so here we turn our discussion of parental involvement to what goes on at the classroom level and what you, as a teacher, can do to assess current practices and to plan for improvement.

We realize that it is important to recognize that the possibilities for appropriate and effective classroom parental involvement strategies vary hugely according to a range of contextual factors, including grade levels, demographics of students and families, school location (i.e., rural, suburban, urban), school organizational factors (number of students, teaming, professional learning communities, and so forth), and personalities and inclinations of teachers.

Obviously, the expectations and realities for classroom-home relationships vary hugely between those of a kindergarten teacher in an affluent suburban school and those of a high school science teacher in a low-income urban school. Nonetheless, for both of these teachers, an equity audit of parental involvement at the classroom level would begin with a self-assessment of current beliefs and practices.

We have developed a brief Parental Involvement Inventory (see Figure 7.1 on page 78 at the end of this chapter) for you to use to guide your own work in this area. The inventory has ten indicators based on factors that research has shown to be related to successful parental involvement.

The indicators are phrased as questions. The middle box in the chart is a space to write your response to each question. The right-hand box, the one labeled "evidence," is a space for you to write down how you know that what you wrote in the response box is true. This may seem overly obvious or redundant, but in our experience of working with schools and teachers, it is not. For example, a teacher may feel that parental expectations for students to attend college are low, but the teacher may be basing this assumption on no data. In other words, the teacher may never have talked to either the students or their parents about college expectations and so may be just assuming they are low, because most parents in the school community do not hold college degrees themselves.

CHAPTER CONCLUSION

This chapter focused on parental and family involvement and provided suggestions and strategies for equity auditing in this area. As with our other chapters, we included the research on this topic and a description of each of the six broad categories of findings that SEDL identified through their extensive literature review on parental involvement. We also included an auditing tool, the Classroom Parental Involvement Inventory, to help you in your auditing efforts. As you focus your attention on equity concerns related to parental involvement, we hope you will keep in mind the major takeaway points of this chapter:

1. Involving parents and families is important.

2. Parental involvement may look different than we have conceptualized it in the past.

3. If we make an attempt to positively connect to our students' families, in almost all cases, they will reciprocate.

4. Caring relationships among the school, home, and student can significantly affect the life outcomes for the student.

The next chapter focuses on programmatic equity, the last topic we address in this book. In discussing programmatic equity, we demonstrate ways of auditing for equity using example programs: advanced placement, gifted and talented, and special education.

DISCUSSION QUESTIONS AND ACTIVITIES

1. For resources and support in improving equitable and excellent parental involvement in classrooms, visit the website of the Harvard Family Research Project: http://www.hfrp.org/family-involvement/publications-resources

2. For an in-depth discussion of parental involvement strategies targeted especially to parents of children with special needs, see Jill Dardig's (2008) Corwin book *Involving Parents of Students With Special Needs: 25 Ready-to-Use Strategies.*

Figure 7.1 Classroom Parental Involvement Inventory

Indicator	Response	Evidence (How Do You Know?)
What languages are spoken in the homes of your students?		
What are parents' hobbies, interests, skills, and talents?		
Do your students' parents have scheduling or transportation issues?		
Do parents of your students feel welcome to contact you?		
With what percentage of your students' parents have you initiated contact (beyond sending forms and grade reports)?		
What portion of the contact reported above was negative (i.e., discipline issues, absences, low grades, and so forth)?		
Do you know where your students live?		
Do the parents of your students have aspirations for their children to attend college?		
Do parents know how their children are performing on accountability tests and requirements for promotion and graduation?		
What are your expectations for appropriate levels of parental involvement in your classroom?		

8 Auditing for Programmatic Equity

Great teachers empathize with kids, respect them, and believe that each one has something special that can be built upon.

—Ann Lieberman

In our previous book, *Using Equity Audits to Create Equitable and Excellent Schools*, we focused at the school level on three facets of equity that are essential in creating excellent schools. These include academic equity, teacher quality equity, and programmatic equity. In this chapter, we address the issues of programmatic equity at the classroom level. Our belief is that schools cannot be equitable and excellent until individual classrooms are equitable and excellent.

There are many areas of programmatic equity that we could examine. For example, we could look at special education, advanced placement, gifted and talented, bilingual education, college readiness programs, extramural programs, technology education, etc. Schools and school districts have a multitude of programs, and there is the potential for equity or inequity, excellence or mediocrity in all these programs. In this chapter we will look specifically at advanced placement, gifted and talented programs, and special education. Certainly all the programs offered in schools need to be of high quality and subject to equity auditing; we believe, though, that looking closely at the three programs we have chosen will allow you to transfer the knowledge garnered to other programs in your schools. For each of the programs, we offer a literature review to highlight current research in the area followed by an auditing activity to help you achieve programmatic equity and excellence.

ADVANCED PLACEMENT

Research

The first program we will discuss is advanced placement (AP). AP courses are designed to allow secondary students to engage in an accelerated, rigorous curriculum. If students successfully complete their AP courses and then take and meet criteria on the AP exams, they receive college credit and/or advanced placement at college for these courses. Moreover, in many schools AP classes count more toward a student's GPA than regular courses. For example, if a student makes an A in an AP course that counts as a 5 on a 4-point scale. So, if one student makes an A in a regular course and another student makes an A in an AP course, the latter student gets more points added to that GPA. This helps the student in competing for academic honors, class rank, and ultimately admission into colleges that use GPA or class rank in admissions.

However, AP courses are not always accessible or available for all students, particularly African American and Latino/a students, including English language learners. This puts them at a disadvantage for college admissions and later life opportunities. Solórzano and Ornelas (2002), studied access to and availability of AP courses specifically for Latino/a students, in both a large school district in California and schools in low-income, urban communities that serve predominantly Latino/a and African American students. They found that these schools offered few AP classes, limiting the number of students who had access to AP classes. Moreover, they found that Latino/a and African American students in more economically and racially diverse schools were significantly underrepresented in AP classes, even in schools in which large numbers of students were enrolled in AP classes. These results suggest that, regardless of the type of school African American and Latino/a students attend, they have less access to AP classes than students in other groups.

Not only do students of color, specifically African American and Latino/a students, have limited access to AP classes, once in these classes they often do not perform as well as their white and Asian counterparts. Additionally, there are lower percentages of African American and Latino/a students, compared to white and Asian students, who take and meet criteria on the AP exams. (See, for example, Texas Education Agency, AEIS report, 2008). However, there is research on the role AP teachers play in helping students of color succeed in AP classes. Burton, Whitman, Yepes-Baraya, Cline, and Kim (2002) conducted a study for their report to the Advanced Placement Research Committee of the College Entrance Examination Board of over 600 U.S. schools with the highest numbers of "underrepresented minority students" taking two of the most frequently taken AP exams: calculus, and English literature and composition. They collected data from questionnaires administered to the school principals to ascertain economic and educational background information on the students and their families as well as information about school, district, and state policies and practices related to AP. They also used questionnaires to survey teachers about their educational and economic backgrounds and their opinions about AP policies in their schools and districts, as well as the teachers' practices in recruiting students for AP and teaching students once they were in AP classes. Additionally, these questionnaires included subject-specific questions related to the AP classes the teachers taught. Follow-up focus groups with approximately 100 teachers were also conducted. Last, this research included student data: scores on the AP exams as well as records of which students took and which students did not take the exam. The findings showed that

> successful teachers of minority [sic] students were good teachers for all groups. They expressed a high opinion of students, both majority and minority, and held them to high standards. They made sure that students understood and could apply the fundamental concepts in the discipline. They also helped students and parents understand and feel comfortable about college. (Burton et al., 2002, p. 3)

Thus, returning to our discussion in Chapter 5 on the Zone of Self-Efficacy, it appears that successful AP teachers believe they can teach all students and ensure that all students are in their zone. In other words, no student is allowed to languish.

Auditing for Equity and Excellence in Advanced Placement Programs

The research is clear that students of color, particular African American and Latino/a students, are not equitably represented in AP classes. Moreover, of those who are in AP classes, many do not take the AP exam or meet criteria if they do take the exam. However, students from these groups are not the only students who may be inequitably represented in AP programs. Your school may have different population groups that must be considered. Regardless, the first step in ensuring equity and excellence in AP programs is awareness of possible inequities. What follows is an Auditing Questionnaire designed to assist you in auditing your class or classes for equity and excellence.

For the questions in the Auditing Questionnaire, consider students from population groups based on gender, race, ethnicity, and economic level as well as students who receive services through special education, bilingual education, gifted and talented programs, and any other population group your school serves. For example, in regard to AP classes, consider the question, "How many of the students in your AP class took the AP exam and met passing criteria?" When auditing for equity, you will need to answer the question considering each of the population groups that are represented at your school, not just those in your class. So, if you are an AP teacher in a school in which 30% of the students are African American, 30% are Latino/a, 30% are white, and 10% are Asian/Pacific Islander, you might not have this representation in your AP class. You need to keep this in mind. So let's say you look at your class, and of your 30 students, 3 (10%) are African American, 7 (23%) are Latino/a, 15 (50%) are white, and 5 (17%) are Asian; this tells you that your class is not representative of the campus racial and ethnic demographics. Figure 8.1 shows a comparison of the school population for the four groups discussed and these groups as they are represented within your class.

You can see by the graph that African Americans are underrepresented in your AP class. African American students compose 30% of the school population but only 10% of your class population. Conversely, white students are overrepresented in your class. White students compose 30% of the school population but 50% of the population of your AP class. If your classroom had an equitable distribution of students, it would look like the graph in Figure 8.2. Therefore, in this scenario, the first important information in auditing for programmatic equity is that this class does not have an equitable distribution of students from each population group

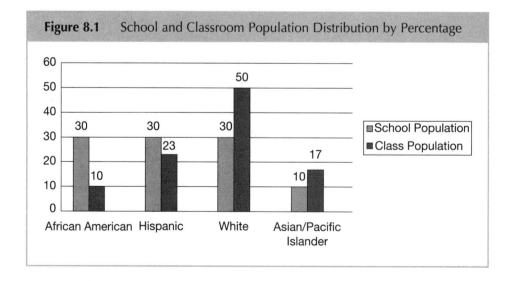

Figure 8.1 School and Classroom Population Distribution by Percentage

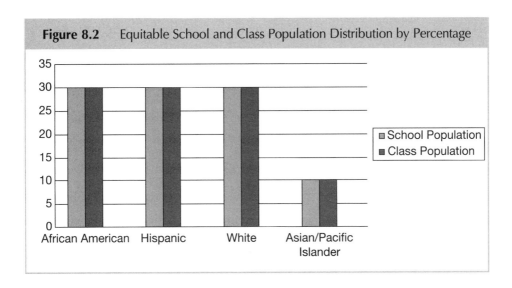

Figure 8.2 Equitable School and Class Population Distribution by Percentage

represented—African American and Hispanic students are underrepresented, and white and Asian students are overrepresented.

It's not enough, though, to just look at the distribution of students within the class; since this is an AP class, we need to look not only at who is in the class but how successful they are in getting AP credit. So, we need to look at how many students within each group are taking the test and meeting AP criteria for college credit. To illustrate, we will look at the actual numbers of students in the state of Texas who took the AP exam in 2008–2009 and how many met criteria on one or more tests (see Figure 8.3).

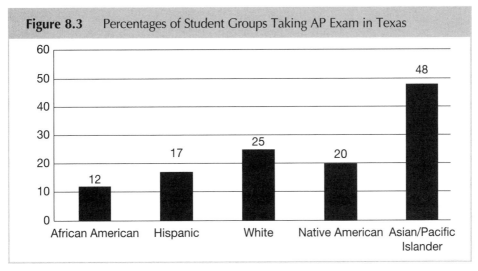

Figure 8.3 Percentages of Student Groups Taking AP Exam in Texas

Source: Texas Education Agency, 2009. The terminology used in this chart is representative of the terminology used by the Texas Education Agency.

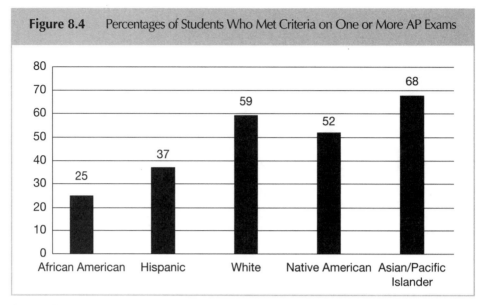

Figure 8.4 Percentages of Students Who Met Criteria on One or More AP Exams

Source: Texas Education Agency, 2009. The terminology used in this chart is representative of the terminology used by the Texas Education Agency.

The chart shows there is a significant gap between African American, Hispanic, and Native American students and their white and Asian/Pacific Islander counterparts in regard to how many are taking the AP exam. For example, only 12% of the African American students in Texas took an AP exam.

Now let's look at how many of the students who took the exam passed it (see Figure 8.4). For the state of Texas, we can see that, again focusing on African American students, because the larger gap exists for that group, only 25% of the 12% of African American students who took the test did well enough to meet the criteria for AP or college credit. That means only 3% of the African American students in the state of Texas met criteria on the AP exam. This is not good! Compare this to the figure for white students, at 59%. That is, 59% of the 25% of white students who took the test met criteria. This means 15% of all the white students in Texas met criteria on at least one of their AP exams. We would contend that this isn't good either, but it is significantly better than the percentages of African American and Hispanic students who met criteria. Therefore, as you consider and answer the questions in the Auditing Questionnaire (see Figure 8.5 on page 94 at the end of this chapter), think about the population groups that are represented at your school.

GIFTED AND TALENTED PROGRAMS

Research

Whereas AP programs address secondary school students, the identification of gifted and talented students usually occurs in elementary school. However, as is the case with AP programs, students of color, students from low-income homes, and English language learners are underrepresented in gifted and talented programs (Donovan & Cross, 2002; Ford, 1998; Lohman, Korb, & Lakin, 2008). This underrepresentation at this early level has significant effects on students throughout their schooling and later in life. "Failure to identify and develop talent in very young children has been linked to subsequent negative outcomes in cognitive, academic, social, and affective development" (Moon & Brighton, 2008, citing Neihart, Reis, Robinson, & Moon, 2002).

There are multiple explanations for this failure to identify and develop talent in young children, particularly young children of color, young children who are English language learners, and young children who come from low-income homes. First, teachers' beliefs concerning the attributes that constitute giftedness affect which children are identified as gifted (Moon & Brighton, 2008).

One myth that has been sustained for decades is this: "The gifted and talented constitute one single homogeneous group and giftedness is a way of being that stays in the person over time and experiences" (Reis & Renzulli, 2009, p. 233). Reis and Renzulli, having spent "more than seven decades" (p. 233) of their combined academic lives studying gifted education, passionately respond that *"There is no single homogeneous group of gifted children and adults, and giftedness is developmental, not fixed at birth"* (p. 233). Many cognitive psychologists (for example, Lauren Resnick) and others would agree with their assertion. Additionally, Neihart et al. (2002) reported on a two-year extensive review of the literature on the characteristics and needs of gifted and talented children and adolescents. They concluded as follows:

> There is no more varied group of young people than the diverse group known as gifted children and adolescents. Not only do they come from every walk of life, every ethnic and socioeconomic group, and every nation, but also they exhibit an almost unlimited range of personal characteristics in temperament, risk-taking and conservatism, introversion and extraversion, reticence and flamboyance, and effort invested in reaching goals. *No standard pattern of talent exists among gifted individuals* (emphasis added) (Neihart et al., 2002, p. 1, as cited in Reis & Renzulli, 2009).

Yet, according to Moon and Brighton (2008), in a study of primary teachers' conceptions of giftedness,

> Greater than one third of the participants indicated that the potential for academic giftedness is not present in all socioeconomic groups in our society, a belief that seriously disadvantages young students in poverty from being considered for gifted programs and services. (p. 473)

Second, in addition to teachers' beliefs regarding the attributes of giftedness that may privilege some groups of students over others, there is a belief by many teachers and administrators that young children in the early years of school should not be identified as gifted, labeled, or "pushed to perform academically" (Sankar-DeLeeuw, 1999, as cited in Moon & Brighton, 2008, p. 449). This may, however, result in students who are gifted and talented being denied interventions that could develop their giftedness. And as mentioned previously, Neihart et al. (2002) stated that this failure to identify and serve these students can have an array of negative outcomes—cognitively, academically, and socially.

Third, the methods and instruments used to refer and identify the gifted and talented can contribute to the underrepresentation of some student groups. Traditionally, teachers nominate students for assessment for gifted and talented programs. However, if teachers' biases preclude them from "seeing" giftedness in some students, particularly African Americans and Latino/as (Tenenbaum & Ruck, 2007), these students may be overlooked. Moreover, even if students are nominated, the instruments often used to determine giftedness are based on "typical gifted behaviors," which are subjectively determined by teachers. Here, again, teacher bias may play a large role in determining who is gifted or not.

Finally, if students from underrepresented groups do get into gifted and talented programs, there is an additional consideration, the retention of these students in gifted and talented programs. Ford and Harris (1997), in a study of African American students in gifted and talented programs, found that some of these students did not want to continue because they felt isolated, either from the white students in the program or because they were the only African American students in their respective programs.

The Auditing Questionnaire for Gifted and Talented Programs (see Figure 8.6 on page 95 at the end of this chapter) is a list of reflective questions that allows you to consider the quality and equity of the gifted and talented programs at your school or in your class.

SPECIAL EDUCATION

Research

Another programmatic area in which there are over- and under-representations of historically marginalized student groups—particularly students of color, English language learners, and students living in low-income homes—is special education. There is much controversy surrounding the issues of special education. Certainly, there are social justice concerns regarding which students are over- and underrepresented in special education (see, for example, Artiles, Harry, Reschley, & Chinn, 2001; Artiles & Trent, 1994; Losen & Orfield, 2002; Reid & Knight, 2006; The Civil Rights Project, 2002). There are also, within disability studies, concerns raised about the medical model on which special education is based that determines who is "normal" and who is not. Researchers in disability studies contend that we, in the Western world, approach "disabilities" and the issues of disproportionate representation of groups of students in special education as a problem to be solved, a technical approach. That is, within this approach we attempt to determine why certain groups are overrepresented or underrepresented and then fix the problem.

Disability studies scholars (for example, Carol Gill, Simi Linto, Donna Mertens, Tom Skrtic, Kim Reid, and Laura Stough) would like us to reframe our focus and look at the historical underpinnings of "labeling," which these scholars believe promotes racism, sexism, classism, and ableism[1]. We agree, and we don't want our efforts here to address the issues of over- and underrepresentation to be interpreted as being merely about fixing a problem without consideration for the sociohistorical context that created the notion of disability. Therefore, within the scope of this work, we will address, although not in depth, some of the sociological, cultural, and historical factors affecting perceptions of disability. However for the purpose of this book, helping teachers audit their classrooms for equity and excellence, we will focus primarily on resolving the immediate problem of inequities in the classroom.

Let's begin as we did with AP by looking at some the numbers. For this section we will use California as our example, as it is a large, diverse state. The student enrollment for California in 2006–2007 is represented in Figure 8.7.

As you can see, the majority of the students in California schools during the 2005–2006 school year are Hispanic or Latino/a and white, with the remaining racial and ethnic groups combined making up only 22% of the school population. However, according to Leadscape (2011), in California during school year 2005–2006, African American students

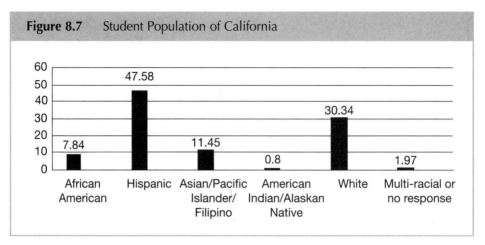

Figure 8.7 Student Population of California

Source: California Department of Education, 2008. The terminology used in this chart is representative of the terminology used by the California Department of Education.

were 1.65 times more likely to be labeled with a disability relative to students in all other population groups in California schools (see Figure 8.8).

Using this same formula, comparing one population group to the combined numbers of all the other population groups, Hispanic students at .99 were not more likely to be labeled, and Asian/Pacific Islanders at .50 were less likely to be labeled. American Indians/Alaskan Natives at 1.15 and white students at 1.25 were, however, more likely to be labeled with a

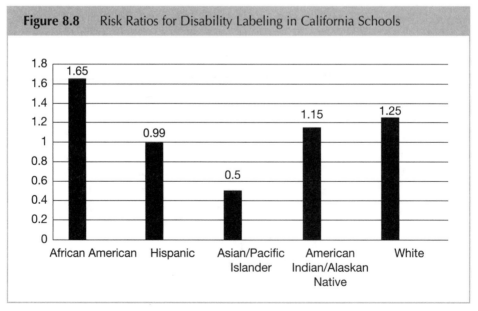

Figure 8.8 Risk Ratios for Disability Labeling in California Schools

Source: Leadscape, 2011. The terminology used in this chart is representative of the terminology used by the California Department of Education.

disability, although much less likely than African American students, who make up only 7.8% of the student population. This tells us that African American students were more likely than students in any other group to be labeled with a disability, although American Indians/Alaskan Natives and whites were also more likely to be labeled.

However, when we look at students who are more likely to be labeled with a high-incidence disability (mental retardation [MR], emotionally disturbed [ED], learning disabled [LD]), the numbers tell a slightly different story. In regard to high-incidence disabilities, African American students were 2.02 times more likely to be labeled (see Figure 8.9), followed by American Indian/Alaskan Native students at 1.20, Hispanic students at 1.15, and white students at 1.03. Asian/Pacific Islander students were less likely to be labeled at .35. So again, African American students are significantly more likely to be labeled with a disability.

As illustrated in the California example, there are certain students and student groups that are more likely than others to be labeled as having a disability. Additionally, some student groups are more often labeled with higher-incidence disabilities, or what Artiles et al. (2001, p. 2) call "judgmental disabilities." What this means is that some groups, particularly African American males, are more often labeled as being in categories that rely more on subjective or judgment calls on the part of the teacher or other adult in the school who completes a referral or assessment

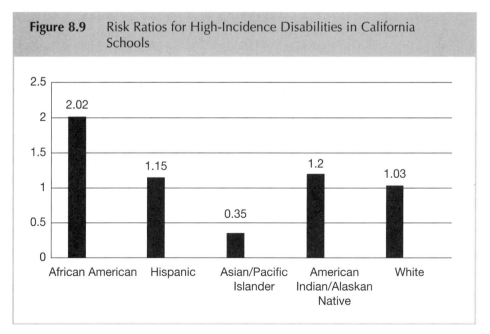

Figure 8.9 Risk Ratios for High-Incidence Disabilities in California Schools

Source: Leadscape, 2011. The terminology used in this chart is representative of the terminology used by the California Department of Education.

of a student perceived to have a disability. Therefore, some student groups, as the California data reveal, are overrepresented in special education and particularly in those areas that address judgmental disabilities. If we are to eliminate this overrepresentation, we need to understand the possible factors that "shape minority representation" (Artiles et al., 2001, p. 5) in special education. According to Artiles et al. (2001), these factors include (1) socioeconomic issues, (2) structural and instructional factors, and (3) cultural discontinuity in referral and placement practices.

First, in regard to socioeconomic factors, poverty can have an effect on children's development, both prior to and after birth. Insufficient nutrition and medical care, as well as poor living conditions, such as living in an older home with exposure to lead, can cause children to have physical and learning difficulties (Artiles et al., 2001; Carolina Environment, Inc., 1999, as cited in Artiles et al., 2001). However, "the effects of poverty cannot satisfactorily explain racial disparities in identification for [such high-incidence disabilities as] mental retardation or emotional disturbance" (Losen & Orfield, 2002, p. xxiii). Indeed, according to The Civil Rights Project at UCLA (2002), "The theory that poverty can explain overrepresentation in mental retardation or emotional disturbance is contradicted by national trends revealed by the data" (p. 2). Thus, while poverty can have an effect on children's development, it cannot account for the racial disparities in identifying students as emotionally disturbed or mentally retarded. In other words, among those who are considered "poor," there is a larger percentage of African Americans, particularly males, labeled as mentally retarded or emotional disturbed than any other racial or ethnic group.

The second possible factor that shapes minority representation in special education, according to Artiles et al. (2001), is "antecedents of referrals" and includes "structural and instructional factors" such as "funding, resources, and quality of schooling" (p. 6). In other words, if funding and resources are not adequate in a school, as is the case in many low-income neighborhood schools serving predominantly students of color, then there may be less funding for instructional interventions, teaching resources, and salaries. This could result in the hiring of less-experienced teachers or a high mobility rate among teachers. All these issues affect teaching and learning. We cannot draw a direct correlation from these factors to the overrepresentation of students in special education, but we must be aware that there is the possibility that low-quality teaching and lack of sufficient interventions can result in increased referrals for special education. Therefore, students who might have been successful in schools with high-quality instruction may end up in special education in schools where the teaching quality is not high. And once in special education, these students may be underserved or poorly served. To illustrate, The Civil Rights Project (2002) found that black children with emotional disturbance often do not receive high quality early intervention and received far fewer hours of counseling and related services than white students with emotional disturbances. The lack of early intervention for minority children may exacerbate their learning and behavior problems and contribute to racial disproportionality in our juvenile justice system. (p. 2)

However, these problems don't just exist in poor schools.

In wealthier districts, contrary to researcher's expectations, black children, especially males, were more likely to be labeled mentally retarded . . . Usually, poverty correlates with poor prenatal care, low birth rates and other factors and therefore an increased risk for disabilities, while wealth usually correlates with a decreased risk. (The Civil Rights Project, 2002, p. 2)

Therefore, regardless of the socioeconomics of a particular school or school district, some groups, particularly black males, are overrepresented in special education and overrepresented in the subjective high-incidence disabilities.

The third factor, according to Artiles et al. (2001), that shapes "minority representation" in special education is "cultural discontinuity in referral and placement practices" (p. 2). Expanding on this point, Harry, Klingner, Sturges, and Moore (2002) conclude that certainly there are differences in the performance and abilities of students, but "the point at which differences result in one child being labeled disabled and another not are totally matters of social decision making. This is the main reason that the disproportionate designation of minorities [sic] is problematic" (p. 72). These scholars contend that there is a subjective nature in the referral and placement process that determines which children are referred, what tests are used, how those tests are interpreted, and what weight is given to particular tests (Harry et al., 2002). Moreover, the results of these tests are presented to parents as indisputable facts. These facts, however, are questionable. For example, one of the most stark examples of the capricious nature of special education labeling, according to Yeselodyke et al. (1992, as cited in Harry & Anderson, 1994), was when in 1973 the American Association of Mental Retardation changed the cut-off score for "mental deficiency" from 85 to 70 on an IQ test, thereby with a pen stroke "swiftly curing thousands of previously disabled children" (Losen & Orfield, 2002, p. xxv).

Beyond the issues raised by Artiles et al. (2001), and drawing from the work of Harry et al. (2002), Losen and Orfield, in the introduction to their book *Racial Inequality in Special Education* (2002), provide a thorough yet succinct overview of the "multiple contributing factors" to overrepresentation in special education. They state,

> School politics, power relationships between school authorities and minority parents, the quality of regular education, and the classroom management skills of the referring teacher also introduce important elements of subjectivity that often go unrecognized. Other race-linked forces at work include poorly trained teachers who are disproportionately employed in minority schools [sic] (some of whom use special education as a disciplinary tool), other resource inequalities correlated to race, beliefs in African American and Latino inferiority and the low expectations that accompany these beliefs, cultural insensitivity, praise differentials, fear and misunderstanding of black males, and over-crowded schools and classrooms that are disproportionately located in school districts with high percentages of minority students. Add to these forces the general phenomenon of white parents' activism, efficaciousness, and high social capital exercised on behalf of their children compared to the relative lack of parent power among minority parents, and one can understand how the combination of regular education problems and the special education identification process has had a disparate impact on students of different races and ethnicities. (p. xxvi)

As one can see, there is an array of complex reasons for the over representation of students of color in special education. Classroom teachers cannot mitigate all these factors, but they can have an effect on many of them. Classroom teachers can audit their practices and possible prejudices. Answering the reflective questions in the Special Education Auditing Questionnaire (see Figure 8.10 on page 96 at the end of this chapter) is the first step in conducting this audit.

CHAPTER CONCLUSION

Programmatic equity is a large topic that spans much of what we do in schools. In this chapter we offered example programs to consider when auditing for equity—advanced placement, gifted and talented, and special education—and we included findings from the research on these programs as well as tools for auditing equity within them.

However, there are many other programs to consider, such as bilingual education, migrant education, extracurricular programs, and career and technical education, to name just a few. Regardless of the program we choose to examine, we need to determine who is and who is not in the program. We need to consider whether there is inequity in student representation and why that might be. Moreover, we need to assess whether within or among these programs there is inequity in curriculum or pedagogy. In other words, regardless of the program, it should be representative of the campuswide student population and be of high quality. As we have tried to convey throughout this text, all students are not the same, but all students deserve an equitable and excellent education.

DISCUSSION QUESTIONS AND ACTIVITIES

1. For strategies and resources designed to support equity in advanced placement programs, visit the College Board's webpage on achieving equity: http://professionals.collegeboard.com/k-12/assessment/ap/equity

2. For resources and strategies to support classroom equity for gifted and talented students, visit the website of the National Resource Center for the Gifted and Talented: http://www.gifted.uconn.edu/nrcgt.html

3. For resource support on classroom equity for students served through special education, visit the website of the Equity Project at Indiana University: http://ceep.indiana.edu/equity/about.php

NOTE

1. *Ableism* is much like racism and sexism. It is discrimination against people who are not considered "able-bodied": those considered "disabled." This can refer to their physical, mental, or cognitive abilities.

Figure 8.5 Auditing Questionnaire for Advanced Placement Programs

1. Based on your school population, do your AP classes reflect your school demographics? Are any student groups over- or underrepresented? If so, why do you think this is?

2. Of the student groups in your AP classes, how many actually take the AP exam? Of those who take the exam, what is the percentage of those who meet criteria? Is there an achievement gap? If so, why do you think this is?

3. Do students transfer out of your AP classes during the year? If so, what population group do they belong to, and why do you think this is happening?

4. Are there students in your general classes or students in the school who you think should be in AP but aren't? If so, why do you think this is happening?

5. If a student or a student's parent comes to you and raises the question of the student dropping your AP class, what do you say? Do you counsel all students and their families the same? If not, why?

6. Are there any students who are in or out of your Zone of Self-Efficacy? If so, which population group do they belong to? Why do you think they are out of your zone? What might you do to bring them into the zone?

7. Do you feel confident with the content of your AP course? If not, why not, and what can you do about it?

8. Are there some students who readily understand your lessons? Why do you think this is? Who are these students? Remember to consider all population groups.

9. Are there some students who have difficulty understanding your lessons? Why do you think this is? Who are these students? Remember to consider all population groups.

10. Based on the questions above, do you believe your class is equitable and excellent; that is a great class for all your students? Are there any areas you can improve? If so, what actions can you take to make these improvements?

Figure 8.6   Auditing Questionnaire for Gifted and Talented Programs

1. If you are a general education teacher, not specifically teaching a class of gifted and talented students, what characteristics do you consider evidence of "giftedness?"

2. Which of your students do you consider to be gifted or to have the potential to be labeled gifted?

3. Based on the students you considered in question 2, which population groups do these students belong to? Consider their race, ethnicity, gender, economics, etc.

4. Are there students in your class or classes that are labeled gifted that you believe are not really gifted?

5. Did you find any evidence of inequities in your perceptions regarding the giftedness of your students? If so, why do you think this is?

6. Based on your school population, do the numbers of students you have in gifted and talented programs reflect your school demographics? (Since gifted and talented students may be pooled together in one or two classes, you may need to consider these numbers across your grade level.) If not, why do you think this is?

7. What is the process for identifying gifted and talented students at your school? Do teachers nominate students? Do teachers complete a questionnaire about the student that relies on subjective responses?

8. If your school relies on teacher nomination, who have you referred for gifted and talented in the past year? Are your referrals representative of the school's demographics? For example, if American Indians make up 25% of your school population, are 25% of your referrals for gifted and talented students who are American Indians? If not, why do you think this is?

9. If your school uses teachers' subjective evaluation of student dispositions for gifted and talented referrals, do you feel confident that you can assess giftedness beyond the traditional characteristics ascribed to the gifted and talented?

10. If you teach gifted and talented students, do you hold all students to high expectations, knowing that some students may think or respond directly to the curriculum more than other students?

Figure 8.10 Auditing Questionnaire for Special Education Programs

1. Based on your school population, do the numbers of students you have in special education reflect your school demographics? For example, if 40% of your students are Latino/Latina, do they make up approximately 40% of the students in your class or grade level that receive services through special education? If not, why do you think this is?

2. If students are pulled out of your class to receive special education services, when does this occur? What instruction are they missing? What happens when they return to class? Are they smoothly integrated into the instructional activities?

3. Have you been given a copy of the individualized education program (IEP) for each of your students who receives services through special education? Has someone who is familiar with each student's program reviewed it with you?

4. Prior to referring a student for assessment for special education, have sufficient response to intervention (RTI) strategies been consistently applied, monitored, assessed, and modified?

5. When a student in your class is having difficulty, do you think, "He will get it with a little more time or a little more help from me"? Or, do you think, "There is something wrong with this student. He needs more than I can provide"? Is race or ethnicity, language, gender, or economics a factor in your thinking?

6. Do you provide high-quality differentiated instruction for your students? Are any students allowed to opt out of learning?

7. Do you speak out positively for students who others may label in pathological or disparaging ways? For example, do you have colleagues who refer to some students as "crazy" or "gangsters" or "freaks"? If so, do you reframe their characterization?

8. If you have students who receive services through special education in your class or classes, do you feel less responsible for their learning than you do for the learning of other students?

9. What do you believe is the purpose of special education? How many of your special education students have successfully transitioned back to regular education?

10. Do you believe that a disability label is something a person has for life?

9 Conclusion

It is the responsibility of every adult . . . to make sure that children hear what we have learned from the lessons of life and to hear over and over that we love them and that they are not alone.

—Marian Wright Edelman

This book has been a labor of love for both of us. We are teachers, and we are mothers. Between the two of us, we have mothered six children. When our children were in K–12 schools, they each had a different experience. Respectively, they were served through special education and gifted and talented programs, attended a special school for the performing arts, and were star athletes. Moreover, one was almost a dropout. Our children had teachers who inspired them and ones who nearly broke their spirits. As any parent knows, getting your child successfully through school may not always be easy or without pain. However, one thing we both know is that our children were the privileged ones. They were racially privileged and economically privileged, and they had parents who worked in the educational system and knew the terrain and how to maneuver it. Due to this privilege, we felt justified in questioning the system when we needed to. Moreover, we had access to the people who had the authority to make things happen. And, we had the financial means to pay for tutors. Today, our children are all doing well. We made sure the system worked for them. We could do this because we had privilege, and so did they.

However, many children are not this fortunate. They have parents who care as deeply about them as we do about ours and as deeply as you care about your children or the children you are close to. Still, having caring parents is not enough to ensure that children get the quality of education they are entitled to. There is a reality in schools that the research and data presented in this book attest to; there is not always equity in schools. Moreover, without equity, there can be no excellence, at least no excellence for all our students.

We addressed the issues of equity and excellence in this book in two sections. In Section I we described not only the aspects of teacher quality, equity consciousness, and high-quality teaching skills, but also conveyed the ways these aspects of quality contribute to the overall equity and excellence in the classroom. In Section II, we addressed specific types of equity audits, auditing for teaching and learning, discipline, parental involvement and programs. Our goal was to extend our use of equity audits, which we have employed at the district and school level, to the classroom level, offering you a practical guide with specific tools to audit for equity and excellence.

In conclusion, we understand the challenges of teaching have never been greater or more exciting. In this time of changing demographics as well as demanding accountability, we can either contend that the sky is falling, or we can see on the horizon a dawn of opportunity. We can say as one group of teachers said to us, "We can't teach these kids. We can't teach this curriculum. It's impossible." To which we replied, "You mean you get up every day and come to this job to teach students and a curriculum that are impossible to teach, and you do it every day? Why would you put yourself through that, coming every day to a job that you know you cannot do?" Or we can say, "We have a challenge. We have the ability and intellect to meet the challenge. This may mean, however, that we have do things differently; we may have to change our attitudes and our practices." As the song says, "Suicide is painless," but change is not. If, however, we are committed to our students, to ourselves, and to our future, we must make the needed changes to ensure equity and excellence for all our students.

We believe in you. We know that teachers are *the* most important persons in the daily educational experience of our students. You, the teacher, matter and make the difference. We are counting on you to help us in this quest for equity and excellence in all schools.

References

Argyris, C., & Schön, D. A. (1974). *Theory in practice: Increasing professional effectiveness*. San Francisco, CA: Jossey-Bass.

Artiles, A. J., Harry, B., Reschley, D., & Chinn, P. (2001). *Over-identification of students of color in special education: A critical overview*. Chicago, IL: The Monarch Center, University of Illinois at Chicago. Retrieved from http://www.monarchcenter.org/pdfs/overidentification.pdf

Artiles, A. J., & Trent, S. C. (1994). Overrepresentation of minority students in special education: A continuing debate. *The Journal of Special Education*, 27(4), 410–437. doi: 10.1177/002246699402700404 1994

Bandura, A. (1994). Self-efficacy. In V. S. Ramachaudran (Ed.). *Encyclopedia of human behavior* (Vol. 4, pp. 71–81). New York: Academic Press. (Reprinted from *Encyclopedia of mental health*, by H. Friedman, Ed., 1998, San Diego, CA: Academic Press).

Barrows, H. S. (1986). A taxonomy of problem-based learning methods. *Medical Education*, 6(20), 481–486. doi: 10.1111/j.1365–2923.1986.tb01386.x

Barrows, H. S., & Tamblyn, R. M. (1980). *Problem-based learning: An approach to medical education*. New York, NY: Springer.

Bloom, B. S. (1956). *Taxonomy of educational objectives handbook 1: Cognitive domain*. New York: Longman.

Bol, L., & Berry, R. Q. (2005). Secondary mathematics teachers' perceptions of the achievement gap. *High School Journal*, 88(4), 32–45. doi: 10.1353/hsj.2005.0007

Brookfield, S. D. (1985). *Self-directed learning: From theory to practice*. San Francisco: Jossey-Bass.

Brookfield, S. D. (1993). Self-directed learning, political clarity, and the critical practice of adult education. *Adult Education Quarterly*, 43(4), 227–242. doi: 10.1177/074173693043004002

Brookfield, S. D. (2009). Self-directed learning. In R. Maclean & D. N. Wilson (Eds.), *International handbook of education for the changing world of work* (pp. 2615–2627). New York, NY: Springer. doi: 10.1007/978-1-4020-5281-1_172

Brooks, K., Schiraldi, V., & Zidenberg, J. (1999). *School house hype: Two years later*. San Francisco, CA: Center on Juvenile and Criminal Justice. Retrieved from http://www.cjcj.org/files/schoolhouse_0.pdf

Brophy, J. (1988). Classroom management as socializing students into clearly articulated roles. *Journal of Classroom Interaction*, 33(1), 1–4.

Burton, N. W., Whitman, N. B., Yepes-Baraya, M., Cline, F., & Kim, R. M. (2002). *Minority student success: The role of teachers in advanced placement courses*. Draft final report prepared for the Advanced Placement Research Committee. New York, NY: The College Entrance Examination Board. Retrieved from http://apcentral.collegeboard.com/apc/public/repository/ap02_minority_pop_11805.pdf

Caffarella, R. S. (1993). Self-directed learning. *New Directions for Adult and Continuing Education, 57,* 25–35. doi: 10.1002/ace.36719935705

California Department of Education. (2008). *Statewide enrollment by ethnicity.* Retrieved from http://dq.cde.ca.gov/dataquest/EnrollEthState.asp?Level= State&TheYear=2005-06&cChoice= EnrollEth1&p=2

Chavkin, N. (1993). *Families and schools in a pluralistic society.* Albany, NY: State University of New York Press.

Clark, R. E. (1983). Reconsidering research on learning from media. *Review of Educational Research, 53*(4), 445–458. doi: 10.3102/ 00346543053004445

Costenbader, B. K., & Markson, S. (1998). School suspension: A study with secondary school students. *Journal of School Psychology, 36,* 59–82. doi: 10.1016/ S0022-4405(97)00050-2

Dardig, J. (2008). *Involving Parents of Students With Special Needs: 25 Ready-to-Use Strategies.* Thousand Oaks, CA: Corwin.

Davis, J. E., & Jordan, W. J. (1994). The effects of school context, structure, and experiences on African American males in middle school and high school. *The Journal of Negro Education, 63*(4), 570–587.

Delgado-Gaitan, C. (1992). School matters in the Mexican-American home: Socializing children to education. *American Educational Research Journal, 29*(3), 495–513.

Delpit, L. (2006). Lessons from teachers. *Journal of Teacher Education, 57*(3), 220–231. doi: 10.1177/0022487105285966

Diamond, J. B., Randolph, A. R., & Spillane, J. P. (2004). Teachers' expectations and sense of responsibility for student learning: The importance of race, class, and organizational habitus. *Anthropology & Education Quarterly, 35*(1), 75–98. doi: 10.1525/aeq.2004.35.1.75

Donovan, S., & Cross, C. T. (2002). *Minority students in special and gifted education.* Washington, DC: National Research Council.

Edmonds, R. (1979). Effective schools for the urban poor. *Educational Leadership, 37*(1), 15–18, 20–24.

Ennis, R. H. (1987). A taxonomy of critical thinking dispositions and abilities. In J. B. Baron & R. J. Sternberg (Eds.), *Teaching thinking skills: Theory and practice* (pp. 9–26). New York, NY: Freeman.

Ferguson, C. (2008). *The school-family connection: Looking at the larger picture.* Austin, TX: SEDL.

Fisher, C. W., Berliner, D. C., Filby, N. N., Marliave, R., Cahen, L. S., & Dishaw, M. M. (1981). Teaching behaviors, academic learning time, and student achievement: An overview. *Journal of Classroom Interaction, 17*(1), 2–15.

Ford, D. Y. (1998). The underrepresentation of minority students in gifted education problem and promises in recruitment and retention. *The Journal of Special Education, 32*(1), 4–14. doi: 10.1177/002246699803200102

Ford, D. Y., & Harris, J. J. (1997). A study of the racial identity and achievement of black males and females. *Roeper Review, 20*(2), 105–110.

Frase, L. E., English, F. W., & Poston, W. K. (1995). *The curriculum management audit.* Lancaster, PA: Technomic.

Freire, P. (1974). *Pedagogy of the oppressed.* New York: Seabury.

Gardner, H. (1983). *Frames of mind: The theory of multiple intelligences.* New York: Basic Books.

Gardner, H. (1999). *Intelligence reframed.* New York: Basic Books.

Gender Equity Education Act. Taiwan, Republic of China. Passed by the Legislative Yuan on June 4, 2004. Retrieved from http://140.118.18.74/files/gender/act.doc

Government of Western Australia. (2009). Conducting a pay equity audit. Retrieved from http://www.commerce.wa.gov.au/labourrelations/Content/Work%20 Life%20Balance/Pay%20Equity/Conducting_a_pay_equity_audit.html

Greenwood, C. R., Horton, B. T., & Utley, C. A. (2002). Academic engagement: Current perspectives on research and practice. *School Psychology Review, 31,* 328–349.

Gregory, A., Skiba, R. J., & Noguera, P. A. (2010). The achievement gap and the discipline gap: Two sides of the same coin? *Educational Researcher, 39,* 59–82. doi: 10.3102/0013189X09357621

Harry, B., & Anderson, M. G. (1994). The disproportionate placement of African American males in special education programs: A critique of the process. *The Journal of Negro Education, 63*(4), 602–619.

Harry, B., Klingner, J., Sturges, K., & Moore, R. (2002). *Of rocks and soft places: Using qualitative methods to investigate the processes that result in disproportionality.* Cambridge, MA: Harvard Publishing Group.

Haycock, K. (2001). Closing the achievement gap. *Educational Leadership, 58*(6), 6–11.

Hewson, P. W., Kahle, J. B., Scantlebury, K., & Davies, D. (2001). Equitable science education in urban middle schools: Do reform efforts make a difference? *Journal of Research in Science Teaching, 38*(10), 1130–1144. doi: 10.1002/tea.10006

Johnson, R., Johnson, D., & Stanne, M. (1986). Comparison of computer-assisted cooperative, competitive, and individualistic learning. *American Educational Research Journal, 23*(3), 382–392.

Johnson, R., & La Salle, R. A. (2010). *Data strategies to uncover and eliminate hidden inequities: The wallpaper effect.* Thousand Oaks, CA: Corwin.

Kahle, J. (1998). *Research equity in systemic reform: How do we assess progress and problems?* Madison, WI: National Institute for Science Teaching.

Kirp, D. L. (1995). Changing conceptions of educational equity. In D. Ravitch & M. A. Vinovskis (Eds.), *Learning from the past: What history teaches us about school reform* (pp. 97–112). Baltimore: Johns Hopkins University Press.

Knowles, M. S. (1975). *Self-directed learning: A guide for learners and teachers.* New York: Cambridge Books.

Kolb, D. (1981). Experiential learning theory and the learning style inventory: A reply to Freedman and Stumpf. *The Academy of Management Review, 6*(2), 289–296. doi: 10.2307/257885

Kolb, D. (1984). *Experiential learning: Experience as the source of learning and development.* New Jersey: Prentice-Hall.

Kolb, D., & Fry, R. (1975). Towards a theory of applied experiential learning. In C. Cooper (Ed.), *Theories of group processes* (pp. 33–57). Chichester, UK: Wiley.

Kuhn, T. S. (1970). *The structure of scientific revolutions* (2nd ed.). Chicago: University of Chicago Press.

Ladson-Billings, G. (1994). *The dreamkeepers: Successful teachers of African American children.* San Francisco: Jossey-Bass.

Ladson-Billings, G. (1995). Toward a theory of culturally relevant pedagogy. *American Educational Research Journal, 32*(3), 465–491.

Laiore, L. (2003). Fieldwork in common places: An ethnographer's experiences in Tory Island. *Ethnomusicology Forum, 12*(1), 113–136. doi: 10.1080/09681220308567355

Leadscape. (2011). *Census count risk ratio (vs. other races), 2005–2006.* Retrieved from http://www.niusileadscape.org/mp/National

Lightfoot, S. L. (1978). *Worlds apart: Relationships between families and schools.* New York: John Wiley.

Lohman, D. F., Korb, K. A., & Lakin, J. M. (2008). Identifying academically gifted English-language learners using nonverbal tests: A comparison of the Raven, NNAT, and CogAT. *Gifted and Talented Quarterly, 52*(4), 275–296. doi: 10.1177/0016986208321808

Lopez, G. R. (2001). The value of hard work: Lessons on parental involvement from immigrant households. *Harvard Educational Review, 71*(3), 416–437.

Losen, D., & Orfield, G. (2002). *Racial inequity in special education.* Cambridge, MA: Harvard Education Publishing.

McKenzie, K., & Lozano, R. (2008). Teachers' zone of self-efficacy: Which students get included, which students get excluded, and more importantly, why. *The National Journal of Urban Education and Practice, 1*(4), 372–384.

McKenzie, K. B., & Scheurich, J. J. (2004). Equity traps: A useful construct for preparing principals to lead schools that are successful with racially diverse students. *Educational Administration Quarterly, 40*(5), 601–632. doi: 10.1177/0013161X04268839

McKenzie, K. B., Skrla, L., & Scheurich, J. J. (2006). Preparing instructional leaders for social justice. *Journal of School Leadership, 16*(2), 158–170.

Mendez, L., & Knoff, H. (2003). Who gets suspended from school and why: A demographic analysis of schools and disciplinary infractions in a large school district. *Education & Treatment of Children, 26*(1), 30–51.

MetLife. (2009). The *MetLife survey of the American teacher: Collaborating for success.* Retrieved from http://www.metlife.com/assets/cao/contributions/foundation/american-teacher/MetLife_Teacher_Survey_2009_Part_2.pdf

Mitchell, J. K., & Poston, W. K. (1992). The equity audit in school reform: Three case studies of educational disparity and incongruity. *International Journal of Educational Reform, 1*(3), 242–247.

Moles, O. C. (1993). *Reaching all families: Creating family-friendly schools.* Darby, PA: Diane Publishing.

Moon, T. R., & Brighton, C. M. (2008). Primary teachers' conceptions of giftedness. *Journal for the Education of the Gifted, 31*(4), 447–480.

National Association of Secondary School Principals. (2000, February). *Statement on civil rights implications of zero tolerance programs.* Testimony presented to the United States Commission on Civil Rights, Washington, DC.

National Center for Education Statistics. (2009). *Contexts of elementary and secondary education: School characteristics and climate.* Retrieved from http://nces.ed.gov/programs/coe/2009/section4/indicator28.asp

National Coalition for Parent Involvement in Education. (2004). *NCLB action briefs: Parental involvement.* Retrieved from http://www.ncpie.org/nclbaction/parent_involvement.html

National Health Service Bristol. (n.d.). *What is a health equity audit?* Retrieved from http://www.bristolpct.nhs.uk/thetrust/equality/Race/hea.asp

Neihart, M., Reis, S., Robinson, S., & Moon, S. (2002). *The social and emotional development of gifted children*: What do we know? Waco, TX: Prufrock Press.

Nichols, J., Ludwin, W., & Iadicola, P. (1999). A darker shade of gray: A year-end analysis of discipline and suspension data. *Equity & Excellence, 32*(1), 43–55. doi: 10.1080/1066568990320105

Oxford, R. L. (1994). Where are we regarding language learning motivation? *The Modern Language Journal, 78*(4), 512–514. doi: 10.2307/328589

Poston, W. K. (1992). The equity audit in school reform: Building a theory for educational research. *International Journal of Educational Reform, 1*(3), 235–241.

Raffaele Mendez, L. M., Knoff, H. M., & Ferron, J. M. (2002). School demographic variables and out-of-school suspension rates: A quantitative and qualitative analysis of large ethnically diverse school district. *Psychology in the Schools, 39,* 259–276. doi: 10.1002/pits.10020

Reid, D. K., & Knight, M. G. (2006). Disability justifies exclusion of minority students: A critical history grounded in disability studies. *Educational Researcher, 35*(6), 18–23.

Reis, S., & Renzulli, J. (2009). Myth 1: The gifted and talented constitute one single homogeneous group and giftedness is a way of being that stays in the person over time and experiences. *Gifted Child Quarterly, 53*(4), 233–235.

Resnick, L. B. (2010). Nesting learning systems for the thinking curriculum. *Educational Researcher, 39*(3), 183–197. doi: 10.3102/0013189X10364671

Savery, J. R., & Duffy, T. M. (1995). Problem based learning: An instructional model and its constructivist framework. *Educational Technology, 5*(35), 31–38.

Scheurich, J., & Skrla, L. (2003). *Leadership for equity and excellence: Creating high-achievement classrooms, schools, and districts.* Thousand Oaks, CA: Corwin.

Schön, D. A. (1983). *The reflective practitioner: How professionals think in action.* New York, NY: Basic Books.

Schön, D. A. (1987). *Educating the reflective practitioner.* San Francisco, CA: Jossey-Bass.

Skiba, R., Michael, R., Nardo, A., & Peterson, R. (2002). The color of discipline: Sources of racial and gender disproportionality in school punishment. *The Urban Review, 34*(4) pp. 317–342. doi: 10.1023/A: 1021320817372

Skrla, L., McKenzie, K. B., & Scheurich, J. J. (2009). *Using equity audits to create equitable and excellent schools.* Thousand Oaks, CA: Corwin.

Skrla, L., McKenzie, K., Scheurich, J. J., & Dickerson, K. (2007, April 12). *Second generation accountability and working class values support system-wide success in an urban fringe Texas district.* Paper presented at the annual meeting of the American Educational Research Association, Chicago, IL.

Skrla, L., Scheurich, J., Garcia, J., & Nolly, G. (2004). Equity audits: A practical leadership tool for developing equitable and excellent schools. *Educational Administration Quarterly, 40*(1), 135–163. doi: 10.1177/0013161X03259148

Skrla, L., Scheurich, J., & Johnson, J. (2000). Thinking carefully about equity and accountability. *Phi Delta Kappan. 82*(4), 293–299.

Sleeter, C. (2008). Equity, democracy, and neoliberal assaults on teacher education. *Teaching and Teacher Education, 24*(9), 1947–1957. doi: 10-1016/j.tate.2008.04.003

Solórzano, D., & Ornelas, A. (2002). A critical race analysis of advance placement classes: A case of educational inequalities. *Journal of Latinos and Education, 1,* 215–229.

Southern Poverty Law Center. (2009, November 24). *'Race to the top fund' offers schools opportunity to improve discipline.* Retrieved from http://www.splcenter.org/get-informed/news/race-to-the-top-fund-offers-schools-opportunity-to-improve-discipline.

Steffy, B. (1993). *The Kentucky education reform.* Lanham, MD: Scarecrow Press.

Tenenbaum, H. R., & Ruck, M. D. (2007). Are teachers' expectations different for racial minority than for European American students? A meta-analysis. *Journal of Educational Psychology, 99*(2), 253–273. doi: 10-1037/0022-0663.99.2.253

Texas Education Agency. (2008). *2007–08 academic excellence indicator system.* Retrieved from http://ritter.tea.state.tx.us/perfreport/aeis/2008/index.html

Texas Education Agency. (2009). *2008–09 academic excellence indicator system.* Retrieved from http://ritter.tea.state.tx.us/perfreport/aeis/2009/state.html

Texas Education Agency. (2010). *Performance-based monitoring division.* Retrieved from http://www.tea.state.tx.us/index2.aspx?id=3846&menu_id=2147483683

The Civil Rights Project. (2000). *Opportunities suspended: The devastating consequences of zero tolerance and school discipline policies.* Report from a National Summit on Zero Tolerance, Washington, DC, June 15–16, 2000. ERIC record ED454314. Retrieved from http://www.eric.ed.gov

The Civil Rights Project. (2002). *Equity overlooked: Charter schools and civil rights policy.* Retrieved from http://civilrightsproject.ucla.edu/research/k-12-education/integration-and-diversity/equity-overlooked-charter-schools-and-civil-rights-policy

Theriot, M. T., Craun, S. W., & Dupper, D. R. (2010). Multilevel evaluation of factors predicting school exclusion among middle and high school students. *Children and Youth Services Review, 32*(1), 13–19. doi: 10.1016/j.childyouth.2009.06.009

U.S. Department of Education. (n.d.). *Office for civil rights.* Retrieved from http://www2.ed.gov/about/offices/list/ocr/aboutocr.html

U.S. Department of Education. (2009). *Annual report to Congress of the Office for Civil Rights fiscal years 2007–08.* Retrieved from http://www2.ed.gov/about/reports/annual/ocr/annrpt2007-08/annrpt2007-08.pdf

Washington Alliance for Better Schools. (2003). A *new wave of evidence: Relationships between effective parental involvement and student achievement.* Retrieved from http://www.newhorizons.org/trans/wabs.htm

Weiss, H. B., Mayer, E., Vaughan, P., Kreider, H., Dearing, E., Hencke, R., & Pinto, K. (2003). Making it work: Low-income working mothers' involvement in their children's education. *American Educational Research Journal, 40*(4) 879–901. doi: 10.3102/00028312040004879

Index

CORWIN

A SAGE Company

The Corwin logo—a raven striding across an open book—represents the union of courage and learning. Corwin is committed to improving education for all learners by publishing books and other professional development resources for those serving the field of PreK–12 education. By providing practical, hands-on materials, Corwin continues to carry out the promise of its motto: **"Helping Educators Do Their Work Better."**